Exploring Education Policy in a Globalized World: Concepts, Contexts, and Practices

Series Editors

Eryong Xue, Faculty of Education, Beijing Normal University, Beijing, China

Simon Marginson, University of Oxford, Oxford, UK

Jian Li, Faculty of Education, Beijing Normal University, Beijing, China

D1739490

This book series explores education policy on Pre-K, K-12, post-secondary education, and vocational education, informing multiple experts from academia to practitioner, and specifically pays focuses on new frontiers and cutting-edge knowledge that transforms future education policy development. It has been initiated by a global group of education policy research centers and institutions, whose faculty and staff includes internationally recognized researchers in comparative education policy studies. The series' mission is to advance the modernization of the education and social construction.

This series provides policymakers and researchers with an in-depth understanding of international education policy from diverse perspectives. Topics include cutting-edge and multidisciplinary studies on identifying, analyzing and uncovering education policy reform and practice among the fields in education policy and pedagogy. It addresses how education policy shapes the development of education systems in different regions and seeks to explain how specific education policies concentrate on accelerating the development of quality education and social progress. More importantly, this book series offers policymakers and educational stakeholders, government, and private sectors a comprehensive lens to investigate the trends, rationales of education policy development internationally.

More information about this series at https://link.springer.com/bookseries/16621

Eryong Xue · Jian Li

China's Vocational Education Reform

Explorations and Analysis

 Springer

Eryong Xue
Faculty of Education
Beijing Normal University
Beijing, China

Jian Li
Faculty of Education
Beijing Normal University
Beijing, China

This study was funded by Beijing Education and Science Priority Research Project: Coordinated Development of Beijing-Tianjin-Hebei Region and Optimal Allocation of Vocational Education in Beijing (Project No.: AEAA17010).

ISSN 2730-6356   ISSN 2730-6364   (electronic)
Exploring Education Policy in a Globalized World: Concepts, Contexts, and Practices
ISBN 978-981-19-0750-0   ISBN 978-981-19-0748-7   (eBook)
https://doi.org/10.1007/978-981-19-0748-7

This Springer imprint is published by the registered company Springer Nature Singapore Pte Ltd.
The registered company address is: 152 Beach Road, #21-01/04 Gateway East, Singapore 189721, Singapore

Preface

Vocational education is the product of social development, the development of human civilization and the product of human development. Vocational education benefits from society and society can benefit from vocational education. Promoting social development is the due meaning and sacred duty of vocational education. In China, vocational education refers to the education that educates can acquire the vocational knowledge, skills and professional ethics needed for a certain occupation or production of labor, including primary vocational education, secondary vocational education and higher vocational education (vocational education at the junior college level, vocational education at the undergraduate level and vocational education at the graduate level). Since the founding of the People's Republic of China 70 years ago, secondary vocational education has trained hundreds of millions of skilled talents for our country and has made certain achievements in personnel training mode, training path and other aspects. The talents cultivated by secondary vocational education are disconnected from the social and economic development and the market demand, resulting in practical problems such as "shortage of skilled workers" and "structural unemployment". To speed up the innovation of secondary vocational education personnel training mode, build a modern vocational education system, put forward the secondary vocational education personnel training mode with Chinese characteristics of school–enterprise cooperation, industry-education integration. Thus, this book aims to explore the holistic development of vocational education in Chinese education system. It investigates the vocational education policy development, student development, allocation of teachers' resources, financial mechanism and system, students' financial aid, examination and enrollment, private vocational education system and school–enterprise cooperation. This book also offers in-depth explorations and analysis of current Chinese vocational education reform comprehensively.

Chapter 1 explores the vocational education policy development trends in China. Since the reform and opening, China's vocational education has experienced a process of gradual recovery and development, which can be divided into five stages: the recovery and establishment period (1978–1984), the simultaneous development period (1985–1990), the sustained development period (1991–1998), the consolidation and adjustment period (1999–2009) and the strategic development period (2010–present). The development of vocational education in China is still faced with new challenges such as the development of digital technology and the adjustment of industrial layout. There are some problems, such as low degree of recognition, insufficient degree of adaptation to industrial development, incomplete school management system and lagging teacher team construction. To better cope with the challenges of the new era, we can accelerate the school–enterprise cooperation and industry-education integration, adapt to the changes brought by digital technology to vocational education, improve the management system of vocational education schools, strengthen the construction of vocational education teachers and other ways to promote the high-quality and balanced development of vocational education.

Chapter 2 analyzes China's vocational education students' development. China is currently in a multi-factor development environment, the upgrading of Internet technology, rapid development of artificial intelligence, the unpredictable international relations and other factors directly lead to the strength of enterprise talent to reach the peak. Nowadays, China's vocational education has been paid more and more attention. Driven by the structural reform of the labor supply side, it undertakes important social responsibilities. As the main body in education, students have become a link that cannot be ignored in the study of China's vocational education. The development of students is a complicated process, which cannot be described simply by data, nor can we see the whole picture at a time node. The research scope of the development of students in vocational education in China can be summarized into three aspects: the input of students, the process of receiving education and the output of students.

Chapter 3 examines the teachers' resources allocation in China's vocational education. With the national economic and industrial structure adjustment and the deepening of the reform, the importance of vocational education in the modernization of the country has become increasingly prominent. The vocational education is a type of education and has the same important status as general education. As the leading force of education and teaching, teachers have played an important role in the process of transformation and promotion of vocational education in China to focus on quality connotation and characteristics. This importance can also be seen in the numerous studies of it by scholars. Through literature retrieval and reading, researchers focus on the following three aspects in the study of vocational education teachers. In the last, the problems and strategies are offered in this study.

Chapter 4 explores China's vocational educational financial mechanism system. Vocational education is an important part of China's education, for China's economic and social development, personnel training to make an important contribution. This study analyzes the current characteristics of vocational education finance based on the data of China's Statistical Yearbook of Education Funding from 2010 to 2018 and finds that there are problems such as insufficient total funding for vocational education, regional imbalance and low level of funding per student, and puts forward some suggestions to solve these problems. Vocational education is an important part of

China's education and an important way to promote economic and social development and employment. Finance of vocational education plays an important role in the development of vocational education, especially in the material security and resource allocation of vocational education. Since the reform and opening, China has carried out corresponding vocational education financial policy reform in different stages according to the national conditions, and constantly improved the financial mechanism and system of vocational education, to give full play to the role of vocational education finance and promote the development of vocational education.

Chapter 5 analyzes the student financial aid in China's vocational education. Vocational education is an important part of China's education, for China's economic and social development, personnel training to make an important contribution. Based on the 2012–2019 Report on the development of Student financial aid in China, this study sorted out the policy texts of student financial aid for vocational education in the past 15 years and found that the degree of funding accuracy was low, education was insufficient, and the source of funds needed to be enriched, and put forward some suggestions for these problems. In the domestic existing research results, scholars for vocational education student funding research content mainly focus on four aspects; First, the establishment and development of financial aid policy system for secondary vocational students; Second, the study of secondary vocational students in the implementation of financial aid policy problems and related countermeasures; Third, the effect evaluation of the implementation of vocational education funding policy; Fourth, we will study the financial aid policies for students from poor families in vocational colleges.

Chapter 6 examines Chinese vocational education exam and enrollment system from different perspectives. As an important part of China's education system, vocational education plays an important role in cultivating diverse technical talents and promoting employment. As one of the most important links in the development of vocational education, the examination and enrollment system has been paid more and more attention by the state. It is of great theoretical value and practical significance to study the system of vocational education examination and enrollment. By consulting the relevant literature of CNKI and comparing the development model of vocational education with that of other developed countries in the world, this paper hopes to provide reasonable countermeasures and suggestions for the enrollment and examination system of vocational education in China.

Chapter 7 explores the reform and development of private vocational education in China. The development of private vocational education is a hot issue in the field of vocational education in recent years. Under the demand of labor force in the transformation of economic development, it is of great significance to study the reform and innovation of private vocational education. This paper takes China's private vocational education as the research object, analyzes the literature on private vocational education on "China National Knowledge Network", summarizes the current situation, predicament and countermeasures of private vocational education in China, so as to better promote the research on private vocational education reform. In China, private vocational education is developed under the condition that education resources are short and cannot meet the social education demand, driven by education demand and market economic reform, and supported by the theory of increasing education supply by realizing education industrialization. As an important part of China's vocational education system, private vocational education plays an important role in increasing the supply of vocational education, improving the quality of vocational education and promoting the reform of vocational education system and mechanism. To some extent, private vocational education makes up for the deficiencies of public education in training talents and promoting educational equity. With the increasing attention and policy support of the state, private vocational education has made great progress. However, as far as the current situation is concerned, private education in China still faces many difficulties and challenges.

Chapter 8 explores the school–enterprise cooperation in Vocational education in China.

At present, with the increasing emphasis on vocational education in China, school–enterprise cooperation in vocational education has increasingly entered the public view and become an important part in the process of vocational education. As important way of vocational education development and progress, university–enterprise cooperation in rapid development at the same time also faces some challenges and problems, based on this, I was in for some documents and policy based on learning and understanding to some analysis on the current situation of university–enterprise cooperation, and for the sustainable development of cooperation between colleges and puts forward some suggestions.

Beijing, China

Eryong Xue
Jian Li

Acknowledgments

Eryong Xue and Jian Li share the co-first authorship and contribute equally to this book.

Many thanks to contributors: Chen Tingyang, Tang Zifan, Bao Chengyuan, Chen Kecheng, Wang Chaoyi, Dong Haoxiang, Jin Hexue, Wang Keyi for their Chinese material collection.

Contents

About the Authors

Eryong Xue is the Professor in China Institute of Education Policy, Faculty of Education, Beijing Normal University, China. Changjiang scholars (young scholars) wasawarded by the Ministry of Education in China. He is also a research fellow of the center for science and technology and education development strategy in Tsinghua University. He is also a postdoctoral fellow in the public administration of Tsinghua University. He has published more than 100 Chinese and English papers in the field of educational research. He has produced more than 100 CSSCI and SSCI articles. He has won the seventh award for outstanding achievements in scientific research in institutions of higher learning, the fifth national award for outstanding achievements in educational scientific research and the award for outstanding achievements in political participation and discussion by the central committee for China Association for Promoting Democracy (CAPD) for more than 60 times. More than 60 independent or co-authored consulting reports were adopted by decision-making departments or approved by leaders. He has presided over more than 10 national or provincial projects such as national social science fund, natural science fund, ministry of education humanities and social science fund, Beijing philosophy and social science project, participated in 9 national or provincial key projects such as ministry of education philosophy and social science project, and 2 international cooperation projects. The project of national natural science foundation of China was awarded excellent. He has been honored as the advanced worker of summer social practice for students at capital college and technical secondary school, the outstanding talent of Beijing division, the young talent of Beijing social science federation, the outstanding talent of Beijing universities and colleges and the outstanding talent of Beijing. Main social part-time jobs: member of the 14th committee of the communist youth league of Beijing, deputy director of the working committee of college students and young teachers, special expert of China education association, China education development strategy society, national academic level office, director of Beijing postdoctoral fellowship (the 20th session).

Jian Li is the Assistant Professor in China Institute of Education Policy, Faculty of Education, Beijing Normal University, China. She received her Ph.D. degree in Educational Leadership and Policy Studies (ELPS), School of Education, Indiana University Bloomington. Her research interests focus on Education policy studies, World-class universities, Globalization and Internationalization of Higher Education. She has published over 60 articles and books regarding China's education policy and comparative higher education studies. Dr. Li currently also serves as think-tanker at China Institute of Education and Social Development, Beijing Normal University. Dr. Li's general area of scholarship is on the assessment of education policy within education institutions comparatively. Within this general area, she has pursued four themes: the education policy studies, globalization of higher education, higher education policy and management, undergraduate students' global learning performance assessment, faculty academic innovation perspective within higher education and comparative higher education development as a framework for institutional research. Dr. Li has published over 60 articles, 20 monographs and book chapters and delivered over 60 workshops and seminars and offered more than 20 keynote, peer-reviewed and invited presentations throughout the U.S. and in Europe, Africa and Asia.

Chapter 1
Vocational Education Policy Development Trends in China

This chapter explores the vocational education policy development trends in China. Since the reform and opening, China's vocational education has experienced a process of gradual recovery and development, which can be divided into five stages: the recovery and establishment period (1978–1984), the simultaneous development period (1985–1990), the sustained development period (1991–1998), the consolidation and adjustment period (1999–2009) and the strategic development period (2010–present). The development of vocational education in China is still faced with new challenges such as the development of digital technology and the adjustment of industrial layout. There are some problems, such as low degree of recognition, insufficient degree of adaptation to industrial development, incomplete school management system and lagging teacher team construction. To better cope with the challenges of the new era, we can accelerate the school–enterprise cooperation and industry-education integration, adapt to the changes brought by digital technology to vocational education, improve the management system of vocational education schools, strengthen the construction of vocational education teachers and other ways to promote the high-quality and balanced development of vocational education. Vocational education, as a professional-oriented education, plays a role in cultivating people's professional quality, helping people adapt to social needs and promoting economic and social development. Since the reform and opening, vocational education has gradually recovered and developed, and a series of national policies have played a supporting and regulating role in vocational education.

1.1 Literature Review

There have been many literatures on the evolution of vocational education policy in China and its driving force.

1.1.1 Research on the Overall Change of Vocational Education Policy

Many studies have made important explorations on the changes of vocational education policy in China from many angles. Qiu et al. (2021) divided the change of vocational education teacher policy since China's reform and opening up into a period of steady progress (1978–2004) and a period of in-depth development (2005 to now); Tang and Zhao (2021) divided the steady progress period into recovery and adjustment period (1978–1994) and consolidation and development period (1995–2004) and called the in-depth development period the promotion and innovation period (2005–now). It also points out that the development direction of vocational education teacher policy is from compulsory institutional change to induced institutional change, from "economic construction" to "people-oriented", and from "single subject" to "multiple subjects". Jiang (2021) studied the change process and development characteristics of the higher vocational education examination and enrollment policy, which was divided into the initial stage (1985–1999), the system improvement stage (2000–2006) and the deep reform stage (2007–2009) and put forward suggestions to improve the coordination and richness of policy tools. It is worth noting that the perspective of historical institutionalism is widely used in the study of policy changes in vocational education. As one of the three important schools of new institutionalism, historical institutionalism mainly focuses on the institutions in history and the history within institutions, showing its explanatory strength in the organic combination of institutions and history. The analytical paradigm of historical institutionalism generally analyzes the deep structure hidden behind institutions from the macro level, including the influence of social economy, politics and culture on institutional changes. The path dependence of institutional evolution is analyzed from the meso-level, including the relationship between the generation and operation of new and old institutions, the ways and paths of institutional maintenance, etc. The dynamic mechanism of institutional change is analyzed from the microlevel, including the power game and rational choice of different actors (Li & Xue, 2021; Wang et al., 2011; Xue & Li, 2020).

1.1.2 Research on Policy Changes of Rural Vocational Education

In the study of policy changes of vocational education in China, the study of rural vocational education is one of the key points, which has been discussed in many literatures. According to these documents, China's rural vocational education policy since the founding of the People's Republic of China can be divided into three periods: agriculture-centered (1949–1978), rural-centered (1978–2000) and farm-centered (since 2001), among which the latter two stages belong to the post-reform and opening period. In the rural-centered stage, the main reasons for the change of rural vocational education policy are the reform of market economic system in economy, the streamlining of administration and decentralization of power in politics and the change of ideology. At the farm-centered stage, the main reasons for the change of rural vocational education policy are the widening of the gap between urban and rural areas, the transfer of rural labor force to cities, the practical needs to solve the "three rural issues" and the influence of the "people-oriented" governing concept. This process of change can bring enlightenments including respecting the law of rural vocational education, strengthening education legislation, perfecting the management system, paying attention to the needs of the educators, paying equal attention to the scale and quality, etc.

1.1.3 Research on Policy Changes of Industry-Education Integration in Vocational Education

The need of industrial transformation and upgrading and personal development has become an important driving force for the policy change of industry-education integration in vocational education. The problems of the policy include the imperfect policy system, the lack of incentive measures, the insufficient implementation, the weak leading role of the government, the imperfect management system of vocational colleges, the incompatibility between the "production" of enterprises and the "teaching" of vocational colleges and the incompatibility between the "production" of enterprises and the "teaching" of vocational colleges. The suggestions and prospects for the policy of the integration of industry and education in vocational education include legalization and institutionalization of policy, improvement of management system, strengthening the leading role of government, paying attention to the construction of the linkage mechanism of industry and education, innovating the governance model, paying attention to incentives, etc.

1.1.4 Research on Policy Changes of Vocational Education in Other Countries and Regions in the World

Some scholars have studied the changes of vocational education policies in some countries and regions in the world and provided suggestions for the evolution of vocational education policies in China. Li systematically studied the changing course of the vocational education policy of the federal government of the United States and proposed the direction of China's vocational education policy:(1) improve the management mechanism, pay attention to the leading role of the government; (2) Consider "career orientation" and pay more attention to students' individual development; (3) Pay more attention to fairness in vocational education. Another scholar, has studied the changes of the Australian vocational education policies since 1990, think of the country's vocational education can bring to our country, including emphasis on quality, inclusive, streamline the management system, playing a role of the market, expanding the scope of the vocational education policy participants, paying great attention to lifelong education and revelation of multicultural education, etc. Wang et al. (2011) studied the changes of the EU's supranational vocational education and training integration policy and pointed out that the EU's vocational education policy is in the process of shifting from decentralization to centralization. With the in-depth development of European integration, the integration of vocational education and training is becoming more and more perfect. Promote the development of vocational education and training in the world by establishing an attractive, targeted, innovative, and career-oriented European system of vocational education and training that is convenient and flexible (Li, 2020a, 2020b, 2021; Li & Xue, 2021; Qiu et al., 2021; Tang & Zhao, 2021).

1.2   Policy Stage of Vocational Education Development in China

1.2.1   *Restoring the Creation Period (1978–1984)*

In 1978, the third Plenary Session of the 11th Central Committee of the CPC made the great decision of "reform and opening up", marking that China has entered a new stage of development. The damaged educational undertakings (including vocational education undertakings) also began to recover. From then on, the first stage of the development of vocational education in China since the reform and opening was until the enactment of the epoch-making Decision on the Reform of the Educational System in 1985. The most important policy document of this period was the report on Structural Reform of Secondary Education, issued in 1980. According to the report, the foundation of China's secondary vocational and technical education is very weak. The document calls for vocational and technical education courses to be gradually added to regular high schools, with subjects to be chosen by students themselves. Some ordinary high schools will be transformed into vocational (technical) schools, vocational middle schools, and agricultural middle schools, and vocational (technical) schools will be set up in all walks of life, and efforts will be made to develop and successfully run technical schools and secondary specialized schools. There shall be special funds for vocational and technical education, and provinces, municipalities and autonomous regions may, considering their actual conditions, formulate specific regulations on such expenditures.

1.2.2 Simultaneous Development Period (1985–1990)

Since 1985, the development of China's vocational education policy has entered a new stage, marked by the central Committee of the Communist Party of China's decision on the Reform of the Education System. The above decision is not specifically aimed at vocational education, but the overall layout of the national education cause, which means that the ruling party of China has a relatively clear overall understanding of the national educational pattern and a basic grasp of the direction of educational reform. Therefore, this period is characterized by the policy of overall planning for education, while the grasp of vocational education as a specialized field is not enough. Vocational education goes hand in hand with other types of education. The Decision places special emphasis on vocational and technical education. The decision points out that vocational and technical education should be vigorously developed. "The Decision" said: The problem of vocational and technical education has been stressed for many years, but the situation has not really opened, an important reason is that the long-term lack of political, cultural and technical preparation for the employment of the people due to the deep-rooted outdated view of vocational and technical education left over from history. Therefore, we should carry out education in the whole party and the whole society, establish the idea that the trade is glorious, and the trade is the top performer, establish the concept that the labor and employment must have certain political, cultural and technical preparation, and reform the relevant labor and personnel system while reforming the education system, and implement the principle of "training first, then employment". Each unit recruits henceforth must choose the best in graduate of all sorts of vocational technology school above all admit. All employees, first of all, professional technical industry employees, like a car driver through the examination to obtain a driving license to allow driving, must be qualified to obtain the examination certificate to go to work (Li, 2020a, 2020b, 2021; Li & Xue, 2021; Wang et al., 2011; Xue & Li, 2020).

1.2.3 Sustainable Development Period (1991–1998)

In the early 1990s, with the Soviet upheaval and Deng Xiaoping's southern tour, both the world and China came to a critical fork in the road. Deng stressed that socialism could have its own market as it developed. The 14th National Congress of the Communist Party of China subsequently set the establishment of a socialist market economy as the goal of economic reform. This inevitably leads to the vocational education to put forward new requirements to adapt to the market economy and society. During this period, vocational education developed steadily and got special attention as a specialized field of education. During this period, there were two important policy documents, namely the Decision on Vigorously Developing Vocational and Technical Education in 1991 and the Vocational Education Law of the People's Republic of China in 1996. In 1991, The State Council issued the Decision on Vigorously Developing Vocational and technical Education, pointing out that great importance should be attached to the strategic position and role of vocational and technical education, the principle of vigorously developing vocational and technical education should be actively implemented, strong policies should be adopted to support the development of vocational and technical education and the reform and capital construction of vocational and technical education should be strengthened; and strengthen and improve the leadership and management of vocational and technical education.

In particular, the Decision points out that in the 1990s, it is necessary to step by step: to make the majority of the newly added labor force basically able to receive the most basic vocational and technical training to meet the needs of the employment position; in some professions with high technical requirements, the employees can more commonly receive systematic and strict vocational and technical education; The basic framework of a vocational and technical education system with Chinese characteristics has been initially established, ranging from primary education to senior education, supporting various industries, with reasonable structure and various forms, and able to communicate and develop in coordination with other education systems. To develop the running of schools by industries, enterprises and institutions, and joint running of schools by various sectors, and encourage democratic parties, public organizations and individuals to run schools; Adhere to the moral education in the first place, reform the teaching content and teaching methods. The document puts forward the overall policy of developing vocational education in a comprehensive and systematic way, emphasizes that vocational and technical education should adapt to the needs of economic and social development and points out the direction for the development of vocational education in China. In 1996, the Vocational Education Law of the People's Republic of China was promulgated, which made China's vocational education guaranteed and standardized by a special law for the first time, which means that China's vocational education is constantly moving toward the direction of the rule of law. This law effectively divides China's vocational schools according to specific needs, mainly including primary, secondary and higher vocational school education. The period of the more important file also includes 1993 "Chinese education reform and development compendium", 1995 of the "principle of opinions about construction demonstration vocational colleges work", 1998 higher education law of the People's Republic of China, etc., some professional policies provide favorable conditions for running schools, it provides some guiding opinions for the development of higher vocational education (Li, 2020a, 2020b, 2021; Qiu et al., 2021; Tang & Zhao, 2021).

1.2.4   Consolidation and Adjustment Period (1999–2009)

At the turn of the new century, some new phenomena and problems have appeared in the social development of our country. In 1999, East Asia was still in the shadow of the financial crisis. This incident made our country's higher vocational education receive attention, many secondary vocational schools in the government's support to become higher vocational schools. However, as the expansion of college enrollment has led to more students taking college entrance examination as their life goal, secondary vocational education has been given a cold shoulder. At the beginning of the twenty-first century, China is facing an important change in 2001, China joined the World Trade Organization. In the context of international market competition, enterprises will have more urgent demand for talents, and economic globalization has promoted the gradual globalization of education.

The change of China's social and economic situation at the turn of the century is an important factor in the development of China's vocational education policy. In the 1990s, compared with China's overall economic development in the same period, the development degree of the primary industry was far less than that of the secondary and tertiary industries. The rapid development of cities and towns and the relative lag of rural areas made the gap between urban and rural areas in China expand rapidly. At the same time, to earn more income, farmers have to work in cities, forming a unique group of "migrant workers". The emergence of migrant workers provides many cheap labors force for the economic development of cities, but seriously restricts the development of rural economy in China, brings "left-behind children", "empty nest families" and other problems, but also increases the pressure of urban management. It becomes the need of rural vocational education in the new period to provide qualified labor force and "new citizens" who can adapt to urban life for the development of urban economy. In 1999, The State Council and the CPC Central Committee issued the Decision of the CPC Central Committee and The State Council on Deepening Educational Reform and Comprehensively Promoting Quality-oriented Education, which clearly stated that various forms should be used to develop higher vocational education and effectively raise the enrollment rate of higher education in China from 9 to 15%. In the same year, the Ministry of Education for secondary vocational education put forward the corresponding guidance, on the layout of the secondary vocational schools have been adjusted, in order to better promote the development of secondary vocational education, the management mechanism, and has carried on the reform of educational system, to achieve the optimal allocation of resources, education quality has improved, for economic construction and social development and provides a good talent pool. In 2000, the Ministry of Education promulgated the opinions on the reform of secondary vocational Education, in which the importance of the reform of secondary vocational education was clarified, and the training objectives and educational system of secondary vocational education were boldly innovated and developed to realize flexible and diversified school-running mechanisms. The regulations also explain the need to strengthen the construction and management of the professional setting, the teaching materials and courses need to be strengthened (Li, 2020a, 2020b, 2021; Li & Xue, 2021; Qiu et al., 2021; Tang & Zhao, 2021; Wang et al., 2011; Xue & Li, 2020).

In the field of rural vocational education, Issued by the Ministry of Education in 2001, the Ministry of Education of secondary vocational schools for rural migrant workers to carry out the vocational education and training notice, request, according to the principle of "actual, practical and pragmatic", the rural migrant workers based culture education for vocational education and at the same time, notice to strengthen their modern production technology, information technology, security Education in production, environmental protection, legal discipline, mental health and professional ethics, and efforts to improve their ideological and moral, cultural and scientific levels. In 2002, The State Council promulgated the Decision on Vigorously Promoting the Reform and Development of Vocational Education, proposing to promote the reform of the management system of vocational education and establish and gradually improve the management system of vocational education under the leadership of The State Council, with multi-level management, local areas as the focus, overall planning by the government and social participation. According to the decision, vocational schools and vocational training institutions should adapt to economic restructuring, technological progress, and changes in the labor market. We should strengthen practical teaching and improve the professional ability of the educated. We will strengthen the ranks of teachers in vocational education. The decision calls for the establishment and gradual improvement of a vocational education management system under the leadership of The State Council, with multi-level management, local leadership, overall planning by the government and social participation. We will deepen the reform of the school-running system for vocational education and form a diversified school-running pattern with government leading, relying on enterprises, giving full play to the role of industries and the active participation of social forces.

The Decision on Vigorously Developing Vocational Education issued by The State Council in 2005 was another landmark document. It holds that the development of vocational education in China has made certain achievements, which are reflected in the employment-oriented reform and development of vocational education gradually becoming the social consensus, the scale of vocational education further expanding, and the ability to serve the economy and society significantly enhanced. However, overall, vocational education is still a weak link in China's educational cause, with unbalanced development, insufficient investment, poor school-running conditions, school-running mechanism and the scale, structure and quality of talent training cannot meet the needs of economic and social development. It made clear that the goal of vocational education reform is to further establish and improve to adapt to the socialist market economic system, meet the needs of the people's lifelong learning, closely combined with market demand and labor employment, university–enterprise cooperation and work-integrated learning, reasonable structure, various forms and flexible open, independent development, modern vocational education system with Chinese characteristics. The decision stressed that vocational education should serve the purpose of socialist modernization, and serve China's new road to industrialization, the transfer of rural labor and the construction of a new socialist countryside, reflecting the importance the country attaches to issues related to agriculture, rural areas and farmers. According to the decision, education and teaching reform should be further deepened to strengthen the training of practical ability and vocational skills of vocational college students. Other aspects of the plan include strict implementation of employment access system, improve the vocational qualification certificate system; We will increase funding input through multiple channels and establish a financial aid system for students in vocational education. It is also necessary to continuously improve the management of relevant academic qualifications, certificates and teacher qualification certificates, and establish a professional qualification standard system that can reflect the needs of economic development and labor market as soon as possible. A major focus of the document is to promote the development of work-study integration and school–enterprise cooperation. In addition, the document said that by 2010, the size of secondary vocational education will reach 8 million people, roughly the same as that of regular high schools. The scale of higher vocational education accounts for more than half of the enrollment of higher education (Li, 2020a, 2020b, 2021; Tang & Zhao, 2021; Wang et al., 2011).

1.2.5 Strategic Development Period (2010–present)

In 2010, the State issued the Outline of the National Medium- and Long-term Plan for Education Reform and Development (2010–2020), which provides an overall plan for China's education reform and development in the next ten years, marking that China's vocational education policy has entered a stage of strategic development. The Outline points out that the development of vocational education is an important way to promote economic development, promote employment, improve people's livelihood and solve the problems concerning agriculture, rural areas and farmers. It is a key link in alleviating the structural contradiction between labor supply and demand and must be placed in a more prominent position. It is necessary to mobilize the enthusiasm of industry enterprises, establish and improve the government-led, industry-guided, enterprise-involved school-running mechanism, formulate laws and regulations to promote school–enterprise cooperation in school-running and promote the institutionalization of school–enterprise cooperation. The Outline also proposes to accelerate the development of vocational education for rural areas and enhance the attractiveness of vocational education. More importantly, the Outline marks that the country places education development at an important position in the national development strategy, believing that education should be promoted in parallel with the country's long-term development, and that education development has become an important part of China's long-term development. In 2014, The State Council issued the Decision on Accelerating the Development of Modern Vocational Education. The decision is a guideline for China to modernize its vocational education system in the new era. Before the promulgations of the Decision, President Xi Jinping pointed out in the 2014 Conference on Vocational Education that vocational education plays an important role in China's human resources construction and talent reserve strategy, and all departments must be aware of the importance of vocational education construction and use all forces to overcome obstacles. Continuing education for employees will reach the target of 350 million. It is stated that by 2020, a modern vocational education system with Chinese characteristics will be in place that meets the needs of development, deeply integrates industry and education, connects secondary and higher vocational education, communicates vocational education with general education and embodies the concept of lifelong education. The decision discusses in detail how to improve the quality of personnel training, including promoting the innovation of personnel training mode, establishing, and improving the curriculum connection system, building "double qualified" teachers, improving the level of information technology, strengthening international exchanges and cooperation and other measures to strengthen the quality of vocational education and teaching (Li, 2020a, 2020b, 2021; Qiu et al., 2021; Tang & Zhao, 2021; Wang et al., 2011). In 2019, The State Council issued the Notice on the Implementation Plan of National Vocational Education Reform, which provided the latest guidance for China's vocational education reform. "Notice" put forward clearly, vocational education and common education are two kinds of different education types, have equally important position. As China enters a new stage of development, industrial upgrading and economic structural adjustment are accelerating, the demand for technical and skilled personnel in all walks of life is more and more urgent, and the important position and role of vocational education are more and more prominent. "Notice" set a target for the development of vocational education in China more specifically. It is necessary to improve the national vocational education system, establish national standards for vocational education, promote the integration of industry and education in the "dual" education of schools and enterprises, build a diversified school-running pattern, improve the technical and skilled personnel guarantee policy, strengthen the supervision and evaluation of vocational education quality and do a good job in the organization and implementation of reform (Wang et al., 2011).

1.3 Challenges of Vocational Education Policy Development in China

1.3.1 External Situation Changes

As socialism with Chinese characteristics has entered a new era, China is facing more and new challenges. Internally, China faces the challenges of industrial transformation and upgrading, transforming the development model, and promoting sustainable development. Externally, in recent years, China has faced increasing external pressure. The US sees China as its biggest strategic competitor and is reshaping its alliances to meet the challenges posed by China's rise. Some scholars believe that since the inauguration of President Biden, events such as the convening of the US-Japan, India-Australia Dialogue meeting, the PASSAGE of the Innovation and Competition Act 2021 by the US Senate, and Biden's trip to Europe have marked the formal formation of the US strategy to contain China with all its strength. However, at present, China's vocational education may face the following new challenges:

In the areas of the economy closely related to vocational and technical education, not only will China's Belt and Road Initiative face challenges, but China's own economy may have to pay more attention to internal cycling, changing the economic system that has been characterized by globalization since the reform and opening up. Such changes, on the one hand, may strengthen the autonomy of China's economy and science and technology; on the other hand, it may cause the Chinese economy to shrink due to the external resources and external space being squeezed. Against this background, the Standing Committee of the Political Bureau of the CPC Central Committee proposed to "deepen supply-side structural reform, give full play to the advantages of China's super-large market and the potential of domestic demand, and build a new development pattern in which domestic and international cycles promote each other". General Secretary Xi Jinping has pointed out that "a new pattern of development should be gradually formed, with the domestic big cycle as the main body and the domestic and international double cycles promoting each other". Vocational education therefore needs to be adjusted more to the type of economy that is geared toward the domestic market.

The manufacturing industry is an important part of the industrial system, and the real economy is the most basic economic form. At the same time, the status of digital information technology in the manufacturing industry has also been increasing attention. In 2020, the fifth plenary session of the party's 19th through examining the "the central committee of the communist party of China 14 to develop the national economy and social development five-year plan and 2035 vision" proposed to put economic development focus on the real economy, manufacturing firm construction power, power quality, network power, digital China, We will upgrade the industrial base, modernize the industrial chain and improve the quality and efficiency of the economy as well as its core competitiveness. This puts forward some new requirements for vocational education, including more effective use of digital technology, cultivating students' information literacy, and promoting the concept of green ecology. As China's economy has entered the "new normal", China's economic development is faced with the unbalanced development between urban and rural areas, the lack of power to upgrade the industrial structure, excess capacity and other problems that restrict China's further development. Under this background, the supply side structural reform from improves the quality of supply, with the reform of the way to promote structural adjustment, distortion correction factor allocation, expand the effective supply, improve adaptability to changes in demand and supply structure flexibility, improve the total factor productivity, better meet the needs of the broad masses of the people, promote the sustainable and healthy economic and social development. This requires vocational education institutions to set up more personalized training programs to deal with a full range of manufacturing categories and adapt to the overall industrial layout of the country (Li, 2020a, 2020b, 2021; Li & Xue, 2021; Qiu et al., 2021; Tang & Zhao, 2021).

1.3.2 Internal Development Challenges

The change of China's macroeconomic layout and policy has brought new challenges and requirements to vocational education. The author believes that from the perspective of vocational education, China's vocational education faces the following challenges under the new social and economic situation: Chinese culture has long pursued the concept of "only reading is high" and "one who is excellent in learning is an official". There is a tendency to disdain labor and vocational education. In China, junior high school students are diverted to general education and vocational education after the high school entrance examination, often only by virtue of the high school entrance examination. Most of those who are frustrated in the high school entrance examination are transferred to vocational education, which in turn further strengthens the social prejudice against vocational education and leads to the decline of the quality of students in vocational education. Due to China's large population and other reasons, the wages and welfare of most factory and site workers are low, which brings the advantage of low cost to China's manufacturing industry, but also leads to the low health and quality of life of blue-collar workers. This certainly undermines the appeal of vocational education. Against this backdrop, the government has introduced a ratio of five to five, leading to increased competition in junior high schools. Compared with general education, vocational education is directly oriented to vocational education. However, the current curriculum of vocational education schools cannot completely fit the reality of economic and social development. The design of training programs in many schools pays more attention to the systematization of professional theoretical knowledge and the correlation between courses rather than practical skills, and there is even no relevant training. Moreover, the professional structure of many higher vocational colleges is relatively single, and the degree of crossover and integration between subject knowledge and skills is not high, which is not conducive to the students trained by China's vocational education system to meet the requirements of compound talents and hindering their contribution to social and economic development. In addition, new technologies bring new industries and new forms of business, shorten the cycle of technological innovation and accelerate the iteration of technology and equipment upgrading. The knowledge and skills learned in traditional schools can only match traditional vocational positions, but it is difficult to match the positions in emerging industries. The overall quality and skill level of industrial workers are not high, which hampers the development of enterprises and restricts the transformation of the manufacturing industry. China's labor productivity is only 40% of the world average and is equivalent to 7.4% of the United States (Li & Xue, 2021; Wang et al., 2011; Xue & Li, 2020).

We have entered the information age, where communication technology and network technology are rapidly reshaping our lives. It can be foreseen that the relationship between teachers and students will be greatly adjusted under the background of new technology. Teachers can accurately understand and capture students' learning situation through artificial intelligence technology, while students can conduct self-learning through the network, APP and other channels and ways. The application of algorithms and artificial intelligence reduces the dependence of students on teachers. In this regard, teachers need to change their role, strengthen students' dominant position and become more of a "helper" rather than a "supervisor". Information technology has also broken the time-space bondage of teaching. The Internet, equipped with a wide variety of educational resources, allows students to learn online whenever and wherever they are convenient, posing new challenges to traditional teaching methods. At present, education is developing toward intelligence, network and individuation. The precise push of big data enables students to break through the constraints of time and space, and the teaching ecology of vocational education is facing reconstruction. However, the current lack of linkages between the education ecosystem and the information technology system is clearly not keeping pace with the rapid development of the information technology system, and this situation needs to be changed. In addition, different online education platforms are "independent", with obvious independence from each other and lack of mutual transfer and sharing of resources. At present, China's vocational education system mainly takes schools as the main body of education, and teaching is mainly carried out in the campus. School full-time teachers are the main undertakers of teaching activities, and enterprises seldom participate in teaching activities. Comparatively speaking, the training method of the school pays more attention to the unified curriculum and lays emphasis on the characteristics of generality and invariance. However, in the real career, the type of enterprise task is often different from person to person and will be adjusted as the environment changes. The lack of specialized construction departments in vocational education schools has hindered the adaptation of vocational education to the reality to some extent. Specialty construction is mainly composed of educational administration departments to carry out before, but with all the professional construction connotation and denotation of expanding the business work, some concrete in the construction of professional business needs by the functional departments responsible for leadership, for example, scientific bureau shall be responsible for the technical skill accumulation, admissions division is responsible for the recruitment of students employment, entrepreneurship, innovation and the personnel department is responsible for the teaching staff, etc. However, there is still a lack of connection between the work of multiple departments. As a department at the same level as other functional departments, the Academic Affairs Office does not have the responsibility of coordination. When encountering problems, it can only seek the assistance of school leaders to solve them, which is not conducive to improving the efficiency of coordination and reducing the cost of coordination. At the same time, the work of undertaking professional construction and training program design of vocational education puts forward higher requirements on the ability of the person in charge, but at present, ordinary teachers who have not been trained usually take up such positions, and the team building mechanism of professional person in charge is still lacking.

Teachers are the main undertakers of school education. The construction of teachers in vocational education is a good guarantee of high-quality vocational education. It is very important to have enough teachers with perfect quality. There is a shortage of full-time teachers in vocational education. In higher vocational colleges, the ratio of full-time teachers to students remained at about 1:23 during the decade from 2010 to 2019, failing to meet the national standard of 1:18. In secondary vocational colleges, the ratio of full-time teachers to students fell from 1:24.74 in 2010 to 1:17.52 in 2019, better than in higher vocational colleges. The education level of vocational education teachers needs to be improved urgently. According to national standards, teachers in higher vocational colleges should have a doctor's degree and teachers in secondary vocational colleges should have a master's degree. However, in 2019, only 36.77% of teachers in higher vocational colleges had doctorate degree, and 85% of teachers in secondary vocational colleges had bachelor's degree, which is still far behind the national standard. Supported by material productive forces, vocational education is related to the state of economic development and shows uneven regional development. The vocational education teachers in the eastern and central regions are in good condition, while the western regions are relatively backward. The number of vocational education teachers in Tibet, Qinghai, Ningxia and other provinces (autonomous regions) is low and their educational level is low, which urgently needs to be improved (Wang et al., 2011; Xue & Li, 2020).

1.4 Suggestions on Vocational Education Policy Development in China

Based on the above analysis, the author thinks that the following countermeasures can be adopted to solve the problems encountered in China's vocational education reality.

1.4.1 Accelerate School–Enterprise Cooperation and Industry-Education Integration

Vocational education is oriented to industry and occupation, and the integration of industry and education is the proper meaning of vocational education. At present, China's vocational education is facing the disconnection between teaching and production, and the teaching and training program is not enough to adapt to the real production. To this end, it is necessary to accelerate the integration of industry and education, simultaneously plan vocational education and economic and social development, coordinate the development of human resources and technological progress, promote education and teaching reform and industrial transformation and upgrading and improve the vocational education form of school–enterprise cooperation. Enterprises should be encouraged to participate in vocational education activities, so that enterprises and schools have the same status as the main body in running schools, and the workplace of enterprises should also be used as a place for teaching activities. This will be beneficial to vocational education teaching and actual production link up. Promoting school–enterprise cooperation and industry-education integration is conducive to more participation of enterprises in the design and implementation of course teaching, so that courses and teaching can better connect with the actual needs of production practice and serve the development of economy and society. The establishment of modern apprenticeship is an important means to promote school–enterprise cooperation and industry-education integration, which requires in-depth cooperation between schools and enterprises, and the joint teaching of knowledge and skills by schoolteachers and industry masters. In order to give full play to the role of enterprises in teaching, the pilot and promotion of modern apprenticeship can be explored and promoted. The Ministry of Education "about modern apprenticeship pilot work opinion" pointed out that modern apprenticeship is conducive to promote the industry and enterprises to participate in the whole process of vocational education personnel training, major setting and industry demand docking, course content and professional standards, teaching process and the production process and docking, graduation certificate and professional qualification certificate of docking, vocational education and lifelong learning. We will improve the quality and target of personnel training. The cooperation between schools and enterprises and the integration of industry and education can also help to reduce the employment pressure of students in vocational education. Recently, the Ministry of Education intends to divert half of junior middle school students to vocational education. However, in Chinese society, competitors with general education and higher degrees are likely to gain an advantage in the labor market, and vocational education is despised by the public. To improve the employment opportunities of vocational college graduates is conducive to changing the traditional idea that "university is the only way out", to the long-term development of vocational education, and to restrain the vicious competition in the field of education. It is also conducive to enterprises' convenient access to human resources, thus reducing the cost of recruiting and training talents (Li, 2020a, 2020b, 2021; Li & Xue, 2021; Qiu et al., 2021; Tang & Zhao, 2021; Wang et al., 2011; Xue & Li, 2020).

1.4.2 Adapt to the Changes Brought by Digital Technology to Vocational Education

Actively adjust vocational education methods to adapt to the digital economy era. Today, with the rapid development of science and technology, new technologies bring new industries and new forms of business. The technological innovation cycle is shortened, and the upgrading and iteration speed of technology and equipment is accelerated. The knowledge and skills learned in traditional schools can only match traditional vocational positions, but cannot match the positions in emerging industries, or the matching degree is not high. To do this, you can build the digital industry talent data platform, through the data platform continues to deepen, tracking digital industry vocational skilled talents demand data, timely and accurate digital industry technology skilled talents demand report, through large data analysis and decision, for vocational colleges professional setting, personnel training plan formulation, the construction of curriculum system and provides the basis for the recruitment of student's scale. Facing the impact and reconstruction of new technologies on vocational education, vocational education should actively embrace new technologies and adapt to market demand according to the requirements of digital industrial structure and talent quality and ability, build a digital professional system that is coordinated with the development of digital economy and connected with enrollment, training and employment, and optimize the professional setting. Taking the construction of professional teaching standards as the starting point to improve the training quality of technical and technical talents, we will deeply develop professional teaching standards that focus on cultivating students' practical operational ability of digital technology skills and the ability to solve practical problems, so as to provide guarantee for digital industry and the transportation of high-quality talents by industrial digitization. Future new learners are "digital natives" and "next generation", their study is more "group work orientation, target and achievement orientation, task orientation, more experimental, highly dependent on the network and experience, love interaction" characteristics, is the study of students' initiative and builder, a discoverer become problem, solvers, communicators, researchers and experts. They need to be fully supported for "high quality learning". To this end, colleges and universities should actively integrate digital technology into teaching design, and use multimedia, online network learning, artificial intelligence, gamification learning and other means to assist teaching.

1.4.3 Improve the Management System of Vocational Education Schools

The school's major construction management system and teaching operation management system need to be optimized and adjusted accordingly. It is necessary to set up a special department of major construction to solve the problems faced by major construction. At present, the Academic Affairs Office is not fully responsible for the major construction, and the specific major construction tasks are taken charge of by each functional office. Therefore, it is necessary to set up a department of specialty construction management at the school level to be fully responsible for the school specialty construction and carry out the top-level design of specialty construction (Li, 2020a, 2020b, 2021; Li & Xue, 2021; Qiu et al., 2021; Tang & Zhao, 2021; Wang et al., 2011; Xue & Li, 2020).

1.4.4 Strengthen the Construction of Teachers for Vocational Education

China's vocational education teachers are still facing the shortage of quantity and quality. In the author's opinion, the state should appropriately increase the salary of teachers, increase the attractiveness of vocational education teaching profession by guaranteeing the treatment of teachers and encourage more excellent talents to join the ranks of vocational education teachers. At the national level, attention should be paid to the unbalanced distribution of vocational education teachers among regions in China. Western China and remote and economically backward areas are extremely short of vocational education teacher resources. More developed provinces can aid these areas, and teachers from these provinces can also go to the backward areas to teach, so as to improve the current situation of regional imbalance in the development of vocational education in China. Colleges and universities can strengthen the training of teachers with the main goal of cultivating "double-qualified" teachers; to encourage teachers to use digital technology, learn more effective teaching methods for practical application, and collaborate to explore instructional designs that are unique to our school. Encouraging teachers to take part in enterprise post training is helpful to improve teachers' practical ability. For new professional teachers, no matter their professional title or educational background, as long as they do not have more than two years of practical work experience in the enterprise in the three years before starting work, they should be arranged to have a one-year internship in the front line of the enterprise. The pre-job training assessment is checked by the enterprise, and the college decides the future of new teachers according to the assessment results of the enterprise. Practice not only enables new teachers to master the latest operational skills and improve their professional ability, but also lays the foundation for new teachers to transform into "double-qualified" teachers. At the same time, colleges and universities can carry out overseas training activities for vocational education teachers to participate in, to broaden their professional horizons. Through overseas training, teachers can learn the world's cutting-edge education concepts and teaching modes, which helps to form a team of teachers with an international vision (Wang et al., 2011; Xue & Li, 2020).

The enterprise is at the forefront of production, with the latest technology and the best technicians. Vocational colleges should also attach importance to absorbing enterprise talents and set up guest professor brand team and part-time teacher brand team. The chairman, general manager and factory director are all top experts in factory management and production technology and can play an important role in promoting the construction of the double-teacher team in the college. The college invites them as visiting professors and invites them to give special lectures or academic reports in their spare time every year to introduce business management concepts, cultural concepts and technical projects to teachers and students, so as to broaden their horizons. The college can also employ technical experts, technical backbone and skilled craftsmen in the production line of enterprises to form a part-time teaching team to undertake the teaching of professional courses or practical courses. Temporary management measures for external part-time teachers are formulated, requiring part-time teachers and full-time teachers to prepare lessons and design teaching situations together, and only after passing the trial teaching can they step on the platform, so as to improve the teaching level of part-time teachers and effectively supplement the double-teacher team. Mutual assistance among teachers should be encouraged. The establishment of professional learning community and teachers' professional community is an important way to improve the overall quality of teachers. It is conducive to promoting mutual assistance and cooperative learning among teachers, thus promoting the inclusion and sharing within the teacher group and promoting the establishment of a perfect teacher professional community.

References

Jiang, B. J. (2021). The changing course and development characteristics of higher vocational education examination and enrollment policy: A two-dimensional analysis based on policy elements and policy tools. *China Vocational and Technical Education, 20* (7), 31–40.

Li, J. (2020a). Compulsory educational policies in rural China since 1978: A macro perspective. *Beijing International Review of Education, 2*(1), 159–164.

Li, J. (2020b). Improving teacher development in rural China: A case of "rural teacher support plan." *Beijing International Review of Education, 2*(2), 301–306.

Li, J., & Xue, E. (2021). Returnee faculty responses to internationalizing "academic ecology" for creating world-class universities in China' elite universities. *Higher Education, 81*(5), 1063–1078.

Li, X. (2021). The process, motivation and enlightenment of rural vocational education policy change. *Hunan Social Sciences, 20*(3), 244–246.

Qiu, L., Li, Z., & Wan, H. (2021). The logic of teacher system in vocational education and its policy implications based on multi-source flow theory. *Journal of Jiujiang Polytechnic, 22*(2), 72–75.

Tang, Q., & Zhao, Y. (2021). Analysis on the changes of China's vocational education teacher education policy since the founding of new China—Based on the perspective of historical institutionalism. *Science of Modern Education, 20*(3), 91–97.

Wang, L., Zhang, J., & Ding, X. (2011). The change of European Union's integration policy of vocational education and training at supranational level. *Vocational and Technical Education, 32*(16), 79–83.

Xue, E., & Li, J. (2020). Exploring the macro education policy design on vocational education system for new generation of migrant workers in China. *Educational Philosophy and Theory, 52*(10), 1028–1039.

Chapter 2
Analysis of the Student Development in Chinese Vocational Education

This chapter analyzes China's vocational education students' development. China is currently in a multi-factor development environment, the upgrading of Internet technology, rapid development of artificial intelligence, the unpredictable international relations and other factors directly lead to the strength of enterprise talent to reach the peak. Nowadays, China's vocational education has been paid more and more attention. Driven by the structural reform of the labor supply side, it undertakes important social responsibilities. As the main body in education, students have become a link that cannot be ignored in the study of China's vocational education. The development of students is a complicated process, which cannot be described simply by data, nor can we see the whole picture at a time node. The research scope of the development of students in vocational education in China can be summarized into three aspects: the input of students, the process of receiving education and the output of students.

2.1 Liteature Review

2.1.1 The Input of Vocational Education Students in China

According to the 2019 Government Work report, "Accelerating the development of modern vocational education is not only conducive to alleviating the current employment pressure, but also a strategic move to address the shortage of highly skilled personnel. We will reform and improve the examination and recruitment methods for higher vocational colleges, encourage more fresh high school students, ex-soldiers, laid-off workers and migrant workers to apply for the examination, and expand the enrollment by one million people this year". In the 2020 government work report, it is proposed that "we will subsidize and expand jobs through training, strengthen market-oriented skill training, encourage workers to take the place of training, and jointly build and share productive training bases. This year and next, more than 35 million people will receive vocational skill training, and two million more people will be enrolled in vocational colleges, so that more workers will acquire skills and find good employment". Under the condition of enrollment expansion of higher vocational colleges, the differences in student source structure of higher vocational colleges are prominent. This year's secondary and high school graduates of higher vocational colleges are the main enrollment objects of higher vocational colleges. Meanwhile, vocational education also undertakes various types of other education, such as adult continuing education, social service education and poverty alleviation education. While the enrollment structure of millions of students includes ex-servicemen, laid-off and unemployed people, migrant workers, new professional farmers, etc., the quality of all kinds of students is quite different. The million-enrollment expansion means that the upward path of vocational education has been opened, and the center of vocational education has been shifted upward, providing a reorganized learning power and more opportunities for upward development for secondary vocational students, even those who want to choose vocational education. At present, the source structure of secondary vocational students is single, mainly fresh junior high school graduates, and still facing recruitment difficulties and serious problems of student loss. From the perspective of students, the social concept makes that students' willingness to choose vocational education is not strong, and the enroll-ment order of secondary vocational colleges is chaotic, and the problems such as the duplication of professional settings further affect students' choice. Moreover, the high school enrollment boom brought by the college expansion makes students more inclined to study in the general high school.

2.1.2 The Process of Vocational Education Students in China

As a type of higher education and an important part of vocational education, higher vocational education has its own unique training objectives and education modes. According to experts, "advanced character" is the benchmark of its training target orientation, "professional character" is the connotation of its training target orienta-tion, and "regional character" is the local characteristics of its training target orienta-tion, and "social character" is the value orientation of its training target orientation. Higher vocational colleges have formed a cluster development structure with more and more complete specialties and higher coverage. But there is still curriculum content emphasis on knowledge introduction light practice ability training, secondary vocational and vocational connection there are also some problems, which makes vocational courses repeat learning and skills training inverted phenomenon.

For secondary vocational schools, one point of view is that the status quo that secondary vocational schools provide low-end labor force for enterprises should be maintained. Another point of view is that secondary vocational schools should return to the standpoint of education and take the development of students' core quality as the basic task. 10 with the gradual shift of vocational education centers, the connection between secondary vocational and higher vocational education has attracted more attention. In the new situation of students' strong demand for high-quality education and higher vocational enrollment expansion, more researchers believe that it is necessary to shift from the final employment education to the transitional vocational preparatory education and higher education. From moral education, aesthetic education and other aspects to promote the secondary vocational curriculum reform to attract students, some private vocational schools in China pursue fashionable courses, but the teaching content is still unchanged. The characteristics of colleges and universities are not clear, the homogeneity is serious, the professional setting is all in a rush, the same and the flood and the talent training is without standard and quality. Therefore, education and teaching reform should be promoted steadily, seeking truth from facts, focusing on students' overall development and paying attention to students' professional quality and personal development in curriculum construction (Cao, 2021; Kang & Fu, 2021; Qin & Chen, 2019; Xu & Yang, 2018; Zhao, 2016).

2.1.3 The Output of Vocational Education Students in China

The research shows that vocational students' employability is composed of five dimensions: vocational ability, independent ability, social adaptation ability, employment ability and innovation and entrepreneurship ability. The factors of school education that have great influence on employability are the characteristic mode of talent training, the teaching links of practice and practical training and the setting of majors. Vocational ability, independent ability and innovation and entrepreneurship ability are the employability that vocational education has great influence on students and students lack. There is no significant difference between the employment rate of higher vocational college graduates and that of college graduates, but the professional matching rate is low, the employment satisfaction is not high, the employment stability is relatively low and the employment quality is not high. Therefore, it is necessary to strengthen the training of students' professional knowledge and skills, strengthen the unit leaders' understanding of vocational college graduates and improve the corresponding work system for the appointment of graduates.

In the current situation, the overall trend of domestic employment is conducive to the employment of secondary vocational students, and due to the lack of vocational graduate's career planning, the school's employment guidance is not comprehensive enough and the deviation of social public opinion, the current secondary vocational student's overall employment is difficult, poor stability, employment quality is not high. Therefore, vocational training should be improved, more opportunities should be provided for students to choose, students should be encouraged to choose their own jobs, and comprehensive and objective employment public opinion guidance should be advocated. The number of secondary vocational students gradually decreased from 22.385 million in 2010 to 15.5526 million in 2018, a total decrease of 6.8324 million. In 2019, the number of secondary vocational students in school rebounded, but only increased to 15.76747 million, an increase of 212,100 over the previous year, with a growth rate of 1.36%. From 2010 to 2012 and from 2016 to 2018, the number of secondary vocational students decreased slightly, while from 2012 to 2016, the number of secondary vocational students decreased significantly. The number of secondary vocational school students in China reached the highest point around 2010. Since then, due to the decrease of school-age children, the number of secondary vocational school students has decreased year by year, and the number of secondary vocational school students has also shown a downward trend. The number of higher vocational students gradually increased from 9.618 million in 2010 to 12.871 million in 2019, with a total increase of 3.1453 million. From 2010 to 2018, the growth rate was small, with a total increase of 1.6752 million, while from 2018 to 2019, the growth rate was steep, with a total increase of 1.4701 million. The growth rate was 12.97%. Overall, we can see that the number of students in secondary vocational school and vocational school is very large, and the number of students in secondary vocational school is always larger than the number of students in vocational school, but the gap is gradually narrowing (Cao, 2021; Kang & Fu, 2021; Qin & Chen, 2019; Xu & Yang, 2018; Zhao, 2016).

The Decision on Accelerating the Development of Modern Vocational Education, issued in 2014, proposes that "by 2020, a modern vocational education system with Chinese characteristics should be established that meets the needs of development, deeply integrates industry and education, connects secondary and higher vocational education, and communicates with the general public, and embodies the concept of lifelong education". At present, China's vocational education system is still in the stage of adjustment, and problems such as the connection between middle and higher vocational education and enrollment expansion are reflected in the development. "Accelerating the development of modern vocational education is not only conducive to easing the current employment pressure, but also a strategic move to address the shortage of skilled personnel", said Premier Li Keqiang in his report on the work of the government on March 25, 2019. We will reform and improve the examination and recruitment methods for higher vocational colleges, encourage more fresh high school students, ex-soldiers, laid-off workers and migrant workers to apply for the examination, and expand the enrollment by one million people this year. "On January 24, 2019, the State Council issued the national vocational education reform implementation plan", including: optimize the education structure, the development of secondary vocational education as a popular high school education and an important foundation for constructing vocational education system with Chinese characteristics, maintaining high school education job than roughly equivalent, make the most of the new labor force between urban and rural areas to accept high school education. … Establish the 'vocational education college entrance examination' system, improve the 'cultural quality + vocational skills' examination and enrollment method, improve the quality of students, to provide students with a variety of entrance and learning methods for higher vocational education. In areas such as preschool education, nursing, elderly care, health services and modern service industries, we will expand the number of junior high school graduates who will be trained through middle and higher vocational colleges'. Through these policy texts, we can see the development direction of China's vocational education enrollment. The following is the change of enrollment in China's secondary and higher vocational schools from 2010 to 2019, as well as the change of their proportion in the education at that stage. From 2010 to 2017, the change and comparison of the employment rate of secondary vocational students (half a year after graduation) shows that the employment rate of secondary vocational students is larger than that of higher vocational students. From 2010 to 2017, the employment rate of secondary vocational students was basically stable in the range of 96–97%, with a small range of change and no obvious fluctuation. Only in 2015, it was slightly lower. The employment rate of higher vocational students showed an overall upward trend, rising from 88.1% in 2010 to 92.1% in 2017, which fell in 2015, and continued to rise in 2016 and 2017. In general, the employment rate of higher vocational students increased relatively large. We can see that in 2019, the number of students in secondary vocational schools accounted for the proportion of the population aged 15–64 in each province. Guangxi Zhuang Autonomous Region, Qinghai Province and Guizhou Province had the largest proportion of students in secondary vocational schools, which were 2.59, 2.39 and 2.34%, respectively. Beijing, Shanghai and Jilin Province had the smallest proportion of students in secondary vocational schools were 0.38, 0.72 and 0.75%, respectively. The proportion of students in Beijing, Shanghai and northeast China is small, while the proportion of students in southwest and northwest China is large (Cao, 2021; Kang & Fu, 2021; Qin & Chen, 2019; Xu & Yang, 2018; Zhao, 2016).

According to Table 3.5, we can see the comparison of the number of higher vocational students in 2019 among different provinces. Among them, Henan, Shandong and Guangdong provinces have the largest number of higher vocational students, with 1,122,500, 1,082,100 and 894,200, respectively. Tibet Autonomous Region, Qinghai Province and Ningxia Hui Autonomous Region have the least number of higher vocational students. The numbers were 10,700, 31,100 and 50,800, respectively. According to Table 3.4, we can see that the number of vocational students in each province accounted for the proportion of the population aged 15–64 in 2019. Among them, Jiangxi province, Henan Province and Chongqing city had the largest proportion of vocational students (2.24, 2.22 and 2.21%, respectively), while Beijing, Tibet Autonomous Region and Qinghai Province had the smallest proportion of vocational students were 0.57, 0.58 and 0.91%, respectively. The proportion of students in higher vocational colleges in Beijing, Shanghai and northeast China is small, while that in southwest China is large. The Decision on Accelerating the Development of Modern Vocational Education, issued in 2014, states that "vocational colleges in eastern China should be supported to expand enrollment for central and western regions, and deepen cooperation in major building, curriculum development, resource sharing, and school management. We will strengthen vocational education in ethnic minority areas, improve the conditions for running vocational schools in ethnic minority areas, continue to run well secondary vocational classes in inland areas such as Tibet and Xinjiang, and develop a number of demonstration specialties for inheriting and innovating ethnic culture". From the perspective of the differential distribution of vocational education in various provincial administrative units in China, we can find that the proportion of secondary vocational students and vocational students in Beijing, Shanghai and northeast China is very small, while the proportion of secondary vocational students and vocational students in southwest China is relatively large. Overall, the number of secondary vocational students and vocational students in eastern China is relatively small, while the number of secondary vocational students and vocational students in western China is relatively large, which may be related to the number of colleges and universities in different regions and the distribution of undergraduate colleges and vocational colleges (Cao, 2021; Kang & Fu, 2021; Xu & Yang, 2018).

2.2   Challenges of Vocational Education Students in China

We can find that the proportion of the number of secondary vocational students in the secondary education has decreased year by year from 51% in 2010 and has been lower than 50%. However, the proportion of the number of higher vocational students in the general higher education has fluctuated and increased. It has been lower than 50% before 2018 but exceeded 50% in 2019 to reach 52.86%. The proportion of students in vocational education is lower than that of students in general high school, while in higher education, the proportion of students in vocational education has exceeded that of students in general higher education. In the current vocational education students development there are still three issues, in accordance with this article begins with three dimensions, this part describes the process and the existing problems in the development of students, the output level is listed in the following problem and has affected the students choose input level, caused the students problems, namely the reason why students don't choose the vocational education. The input problem is the reflection of the result that students do not choose vocational education.

Many colleges and universities, regardless of their own conditions, set up a rush to follow the "market", catch up with the fashion of the "high" professional, in order to attract the attention of the community and parents, to give themselves gold; When the limelight has passed, these majors have become the past, and will not hesitate to abandon these majors, some in the limelight of the new "hot professional". According to the Ministry of Education, 207 out of 1,423 higher vocational colleges and universities offer the major of "cloud computing Technology and Application", 399 have the major of "Big Data Technology and Application", 498 have the major of "Internet of Things Application Technology" and 568 have the major of "Industrial Robot Technology". Colleges and universities offering the above majors, respectively, account for 14.6, 28, 35 and 40% of the total number of higher vocational (junior college) colleges. The following set of professional and original major difference is not obvious, because the schoolteachers focus on these areas in a short time, designed in line with market demand of professional courses, these professionals only stay in the name of "tall", the actual content is not much progress, hard to fit the actual needs of the market, still can't solve the fundamental problem (Cao, 2021; Kang & Fu, 2021; Qin & Chen, 2019; Xu & Yang, 2018; Zhao, 2016).

On the one hand, some vocational colleges have outdated campus facilities and backward hardware facilities, which cannot be well connected with enterprises, nor can they provide students with good training conditions or internship opportunities, so students' willingness is relatively low. In addition, many vocational colleges and universities are in chaos and there is a scramble for students, which makes students or parents have a defensive attitude in the process of choosing vocational education. There has been a study on some vocational students, which shows that students in school reflect a problem, that is, vocational colleges cannot provide vocational education for students well, in the study, few students think that they have really learned technology during school. 14 Secondary vocational schools also have similar problems. Secondary vocational schools even take the proportion of students entering higher vocational schools as the data of school publicity, which indicates that at present secondary vocational schools do not regard the social and professional development of students as the primary goal, but close to the direction of non-vocational education. On the other hand, due to the low level of students, students' learning desire is not high, the overall quality is low, and the learning atmosphere is not strong, which on the other hand, has affected the teachers' teaching enthusiasm, students in school is difficult to form the learning organization outside the classroom, informal learning is less, in the actual vocational school recruit students, there are also students tend to vocational education, but because the score is too low, vocational colleges students would not like to waste points or cannot accept the poor quality of students. Therefore, neither students nor parents are inclined to choose vocational colleges.

2.2.1 The Difficulty of Entering Higher Education After Receiving Vocational Education

Although vocational school students have a variety of pathways to further their studies, they are not recognized by the mainstream and are not connected with the general education, making it difficult for students to continue their studies. Moreover, the society generally cannot give skilled talents a higher social status, so students have many concerns when choosing vocational education. In the public opinion of the society, vocational education is often synonymous with poor study, and choosing vocational education is usually the last choice after failing to go to school. In such a situation, students with better study usually do not choose vocational education but choose to continue their studies in ordinary high school or university. However, vocational education is discriminated by society to some extent and cannot well meet the demands of most students for educational results. On the other hand, in the actual employment process in the market, the employment rate of students and the satisfaction of employers have improved compared with before, but the problem of talent skills mismatch still exists. In the current grim employment situation, this has a hindering effect on students' choice of vocational education. Vocational education graduates have strong operational skills, good professional spirit and working attitude, but there are problems such as narrow knowledge and lack of independent innovation ability. Their professional theory level is basically adapted to the job, but there are still deficiencies. In addition, there is a large gap in the level of graduates produced by vocational education. From the perspective of individuals, it can be found that the individual difference of vocational education graduates is large, which is derived from the level of vocational schools on the one hand and the individual difference of students on the other. Because our country industry transformation acceleration, the demand of talents of high-quality workers and high technical skills continue to increase, and at the same time, advanced technical skills talents effective supply is insufficient, skilled workers in our country in all employment accounted for less than 20% of the population, in the skilled workers, accounts for less than 5% of the talent of high technical skills. There is a shortage of senior skilled workers in many units. However, due to the long training period and the large job mobility of graduates, the units do not tend to train graduates directly. On the contrary, the degree of matching between graduates' jobs and their majors is low, and the vocational education they receive cannot be well used, resulting in a waste of resources (Qin & Chen, 2019; Zhao, 2016).

2.2.2 The Reflection that Students Do Not Choose Vocational Education

By 2019, there were 40.2 million students in higher education, with the gross enrollment rate reaching 51.6%. In just 20 years, China's higher education has entered the popularization stage at an amazing speed, and higher vocational education has played a vital role. In 2019, 4.836,100 students enrolled in higher vocational colleges and colleges, accounting for 52.85% of the total, exceeding the undergraduate enrollment for the first time in history. According to the 2017 talent blue book "China Talent Development Report (No.4)" released by The Social Sciences Academic Press, China has a shortage of 10 million senior skilled workers, and only 5% of the industrial workers are above senior level. The number of skilled workers in China accounts for 19% of the total number of employed people, while highly skilled people account for only 5%, according to a study on The Skill Gap in China's Labor Market published in 2016. Of the nearly 280 million migrant workers in 2015, only 0.3% had been trained to work. The overall quality and skill level of industrial workers are not high, which hampers the development of enterprises and restricts the transformation of the manufacturing industry. China's labor productivity is only 40% of the world average and equivalent to 7.4% of the United States. Vocational education, which has been low level, extensive and large-scale expansion for many years, cannot complete the transformation of school-running and connotation construction in a short period of time, and falls into the self-development dilemma of "too big to be dropped". It is in urgent need of supply-side reform of vocational education. Under the influence of the bad social atmosphere of eager for quick success and cheap labor, the social recognition of vocational education is low and is seriously despised. Students, parents and enterprises do not like it and do not look forward to it. Vocational colleges themselves cannot escape the blame, and the supply-side reform of vocational education is urgent. The key point for secondary vocational schools to attract all kinds of students is to effectively enhance the application skills training and employment competitiveness of secondary vocational education and provide smooth channels of higher education admission for secondary vocational school graduates and opportunities comparable with ordinary high schools (Qin & Chen, 2019; Xu & Yang, 2018; Zhao, 2016).

To sum up, these problems still exist are caused by the nature of vocational education. These problems exist now and may persist for a long time. They can only be alleviated to a certain extent but cannot be solved completely. Furthermore, vocational education is required to provide a higher level of education. However, due to the lag of education itself, there is a certain gap between the implementation of educational policies and their effectiveness. Despite the intervention of existing policies, it is difficult to require education to always meet the requirements of The Times due to the rapid development of society. The fourth part will combine the existing problems and previous research experience and put forward several policy suggestions.

2.3 Suggestions on Vocational Education Students in China

Corresponding to the third part, this paper puts forward several policy suggestions to solve the problem that students do not choose vocational education. At present, there are existing policies to alleviate these problems. Therefore, the suggestions put forward in this paper are to continue the current existing policies, continue to implement and implement the current policies and provide some improvement strategies. The first two suggestions focus on schools and the alliance between schools and enterprises, while the third one puts forward suggestions from the perspective of comprehensive results and puts forward countermeasures for problems in the ideological field.

2.3.1 Integration of Production and Education

First, it provides suggestions on the process of vocational education from the perspective of production-education integration. This perspective is to promote the integration of industry and education, improve the matching degree of students' ability and market requirements, and then promote the development of students. To promote the integration of vocational education and market demand, industry-education integration can effectively improve the effect of vocational education, promote talent training and college development and improve the degree of conformity between talent ability and market demand, and its effect is widely recognized. The policy should continue the idea of both schools and enterprises as a "community with a shared future" mentioned in the implementation Plan of National Vocational Education Reform in 2019, pay attention to the specific demands of various stakeholders, and pay attention to the coordination and power distribution among various departments and stakeholders in the process of policy implementation. Policies have a great influence on the implementation of production-education integration. There exist some problems in the current policy in the process of execution, such as the policy execution subject value appeal conflict, inconsistent policy targets, the relationship between the inter-ministerial fragmentation and other issues, so we need to balance the interests of all parties, resulting in the main body to be able to participate in policy formulation and perfection, to better promote the implementation of the existing policy. Therefore, to better promote the integration of industry and education, specific policies can provide incentives for enterprises, such as releasing the right to run schools, giving preferential fiscal and tax policies to enterprises, so as to promote enterprises to strengthen cooperation, promote the integration of industry and education and encourage enterprises to participate more in vocational education.

For example, in terms of policy, it is necessary to establish a benefit compensation mechanism for enterprises to participate in vocational education, and the government should stipulate those enterprises of a certain scale must undertake the responsibility of participating in vocational education in the form of school–enterprise cooperation. Because the tester is the enterprise of professional education eventually, so if you want to promote students' employment competitiveness and professional ability, it requires vocational colleges will be part of the right to the enterprise, such ability can improve the enthusiasm of enterprises to participate in the integration between production, in addition, you also need to convection between vocational colleges and enterprises to realize talents, discuss common objectives, Jointly build curriculum system and assessment scheme. The empirical study shows that "decentralization" can well stimulate the enthusiasm of enterprises to participate in school–enterprise cooperation. At present, there are preferential policies for enterprises to participate in school–enterprise cooperation, but the policies still lack authority, rationality and operability, and some guiding policies are not mandatory, and cannot really make enterprises gain benefits, so their role is not obvious. To sum up, in terms of policy formulation and improvement, China needs to continue to improve the policy support system that encourages enterprises to participate in school–enterprise cooperation (Cao, 2021; Kang & Fu, 2021; Qin & Chen, 2019; Xu & Yang, 2018; Zhao, 2016).

2.3.2 School Construction

From the perspective of school construction, it provides suggestions for the main body of vocational education. This perspective is to promote vocational education entities to improve their own level, to provide students with a broader space for development and learning environment. In terms of school construction, schools should implement and promote the reform of "three education", build a high level of "double qualified" teachers, create distinctive vocational teaching materials and innovate teaching methods with classroom revolution as the core. The formulation and improvement of policies should facilitate the reform of colleges and universities and encourage colleges and universities to improve their training mode and talent development path according to social needs, so that they can better meet social needs and produce talents. Specifically, policies should promote the implementation of the "double-qualified" teacher training project, comprehensively improve the quality of double-qualified teachers and establish the "double-qualified" teacher standards recognized by the government, industry and enterprises. The government should introduce policies on the personnel training system, improve the support for high-level personnel training and strengthen the incentive and reward measures for talents, promote the implementation of the reform of the personnel development system and mechanism and the introduction of personnel training and use policies to attract leading scientific research talents and skilled craftsmen into the teaching staff.

Government also should keep overall planning, rational planning of vocational education, scientific planning, encourage vocational skills competition policy, strengthen the infrastructure construction of vocational education, improving the quality of vocational colleges, strictly regulate the recruitment of students order, adjust professional structure, encourage various colleges and universities according to their actual build professional backbone, forming the professional features. We will strictly control the enrollment plan, and strictly inspect and punish any behavior that disrupts the enrollment order. At the same time, the senior high school restriction policy should be scientifically formulated, and the strict supervision and implementation should be carried out to provide the source of students for vocational education. In addition, the need to encourage the development of school characteristics, according to regional type because of vocational colleges is to support regional economic and social development demand and birth, development, types of regional economic development is a vocational colleges, the characteristics of the development of the internal driving force, thus to promote the development of vocational school characteristics, to strengthen the construction of teachers team. Through the teacher's credentials the exercise under the enterprise, to leave a variety of forms such as entrepreneurship, enterprise craftsmen into classroom, increase liquidity vocational colleges teachers, let the school full-time teachers master the enterprise new changes, the standard of choosing and employing persons, new technology and new products, update their professional knowledge and practical skills experience, let part-time teachers are familiar with the whole process of talent cultivation, bring practical technical skills to the classroom. The government needs to increase the public financial input in vocational education and conduct cost accounting of personnel training, set up special funds for key major reform of vocational education, guide vocational colleges to grasp the real connotation construction and expand diversified financing channels for vocational colleges.

2.3.3   Social Values

From the perspective of the overall occupational view of the society, there are still existing serious labor problems, such as the present social values. And we found that the society is not a good place to receive vocational education and we need to establish a good and qualified professional education pathway to cultivate vocational talents in the current education system.

To be specific, policy support is needed to guarantee the salary level of technical talents. In addition to the salary level of top technical talents, the salary level of medium or ordinary skilled workers should also be paid attention to, so that students receiving vocational education can get better opportunities after graduation. In addition, it is necessary to increase the guidance of the news media, strengthen the encouragement of technical talents in the society and provide economic rewards for them, to improve the social understanding of vocational education. The same needs to be done to promote vocational schools and instill people with the idea that vocational education is not necessarily of poor quality. We should vigorously advocate the "craftsman spirit" and create a trend of The Times that labor is glorious, and skills are valuable. The public should have a clearer understanding of the professional setting, development direction and training mode of vocational education, so that students and their parents can choose vocational education more targeted. The most fundamental way to change social values is to change the existing enrollment standards of vocational education. First, students who want to receive vocational education should be able to make a free choice when they enter the system, rather than being forced to choose vocational education because of their lack of academic performance. Instead of admitting students who do not do well in the high school entrance exam or the Gaokao, a selection system that can stand alongside general education needs to be established. Next, it can promote vocational colleges and colleges of undergraduate course of common senior high school or class communication, on the one hand, strengthen the teaching of cultural quality of the vocational colleges, on the other hand for ordinary education system of the students with the chance to know more about vocational education, school choice to provide more information for the future, at the same time reduce the bias for vocational education. Moreover, the differentiated competition between higher vocational education and ordinary undergraduate education should be encouraged to enhance the social identity of higher vocational education. In fact, the impression of social values on vocational education not only comes from the continuation of thought, but also from the objective performance of vocational education and the prejudice caused by incomplete information. If we want to change the social value of vocational education, we should start with the guidance of public opinion environment, objective construction of vocational education and more comprehensive publicity to guide and respect the value orientation of vocational education (Cao, 2021; Kang & Fu, 2021; Qin & Chen, 2019; Xu & Yang, 2018; Zhao, 2016).

References

Cao, Q. (2021). Problems and paths of training double-qualified teachers in western higher vocational colleges. *Education and Employment, 20*(10), 82–85.

Kang, L., & Fu, Y. (2021). Research and practice on the construction of talents training highland in higher vocational colleges. *Vocational Technology, 20*(8), 58–62.

Qin, H. W., & Chen, G. (2019). "Three education" reform under the background of "double-high plan". *China Vocational and Technical Education, 40*(33), 35–38.

Xu, S., & Yang, J. (2018). How to implement enterprises' dominant position in vocational education school-enterprise cooperation: An empirical analysis based on incentive effect. *China Vocational and Technical Education, 20*(6), 31–38.

Zhao, H. (2016). Research on the reasons, obstacles and promoting policies of enterprises' participation in vocational education school-enterprise cooperation. *Vocational Education Forum, 20*(9), 46–50.

References

Chapter 3
The Allocation of Teachers' Resources in China's Vocational Education

This chapter examines the teachers' resources allocation in China's vocational education. With the national economic and industrial structure adjustment and the deepening of the reform, the importance of vocational education in the modernization of the country has become increasingly prominent. The vocational education is a type of education and has the same important status as general education. As the leading force of education and teaching, teachers have played an important role in the process of transformation and promotion of vocational education in China to focus on quality connotation and characteristics. This importance can also be seen in the numerous studies of it by scholars. Through literature retrieval and reading, researchers focus on the following three aspects in the study of vocational education teachers. In the last, the problems and strategies are offered in this study.

3.1 Literature Review

3.1.1 Research on Teacher Policy in Vocational Education

Policy plays an important role in regulating and guaranteeing, and a scientific and reasonable vocational education teacher policy system is of great significance for promoting the development of vocational education teachers. Studies on teacher policies in vocational education are mainly divided into two categories: The first category analyzes the number, type, content, deficiency and improvement direction of China's vocational education teacher policies by reviewing and combing them. Gong (2012) through to the text about vocational education teachers since the reform and opening up policy of carding and analysis, found that has built in China, including comprehensive policies, qualification and employment policies, training, pay and reward policy, the policy system of vocational education teachers, but the system is not perfect enough, there is "deficiency" and "old" two big problems, Some thoughts and suggestions are put forward accordingly.

Wang et al. (2021) sorted out and analyzed relevant policies according to the four stages of recovery and reconstruction, reform exploration, optimization and adjustment, and deepening development, based on the social development background and the promulgations of major policies. On this basis, they reflected on the deficiencies of policies and put forward suggestions. The other is to study a certain aspect of vocational education teachers in the background of vocational education teacher policies. This kind of article mainly focuses on the analysis of vocational education teachers, but also involves the sorting and analysis of relevant policies. Li (2014), through sorting out the policies of "double-qualified" teachers, believes that the connotation of "double-qualified" teachers is in constant change, generally pointing to four stages, each stage is different, and analyzes the positioning of teachers of public courses, professional courses and practice guidance in vocational education. Yang et al. (2021) studied the secondary vocational education teacher training under the 1 + X certificate system and analyzed the achievements and improvement suggestions of the secondary vocational education teacher training in China. From the perspective of the research content of the policy of vocational education teachers, the researchers focused on the evolution of China's vocational education teacher policy process, pay attention to a review of the policy and comb, constantly explore the rationality of the policy system and the concrete policy and deficiencies, to do a lot of policy text analysis, but the focus of policy implementation and effects. From the perspective of research methods, the research on vocational education teacher policy is more theoretical than empirical, which is also related to the tendency of research content.

3.1.2   Research on "Double-Qualified" Vocational Education Teachers

Scholars have paid much attention to the study of "double-qualified" teachers. In the CNKI "vocational education teacher research" as the topic of search, search results appeared a lot of "double qualified" teachers' content; If we search the subject of "double-qualified", there are 11,700 academic journals and 436 dissertations. It can be seen that "double-qualified" teachers are indeed a hot spot in the research of vocational education teachers. The concept of "double-qualified" teachers has existed for a long time. It was rooted in the historical environment of severe shortage of skilled teachers in the transition from ordinary high schools to vocational high schools in the early 1980s. It was formed in the practice of vocational colleges in the late 1980s and early 1990s, and officially appeared in the official documents in the mid-1990s.

The research on "double-qualified" teachers can be roughly divided into two categories. The first is the interpretation of "double teacher". Yao (2002) introduced several common misunderstandings about "double-qualified" teachers in vocational education and put forward the basic competence and professional competence that "double-qualified" teachers should possess. Xiao and Zhang defined the concept of "double-qualified" teachers by analyzing and reflecting on the expressions of "double-qualified" teachers in policy documents and scholars. Shi et al. (2021) put forward "three teachers" on top of "double teachers", emphasizing the importance of application-oriented and development-oriented scientific research on teacher development in vocational education. The second is to explore the construction of vocational education teachers from the perspective of "double-qualified" teachers, including the composition structure, construction path, construction effect and so on. Cao (2021) analyzed the effectiveness of the construction of vocational education teachers in China during the 13th Five-Year Plan period and prospected the 14th Five-year Plan period, which also involved the construction of "double-qualified" teachers for many times. Due to the policy in the text puts forward the concept of "double type" teachers did not give a specific explanation, interpreting the connotation of the "double type" teachers is always the key point of the research, the connotation of "double type" teachers with the deepening of the development of The Times and the research also gradually rich, formed the "double certificate", "double title", "double quality", etc. In addition to the interpretation of "double-qualified" teachers, the emergence of "double-qualified" teachers should have the ability, quality and the construction of teacher team research naturally, mostly through the macro perspective to analyze the problem. This part of research often focuses on the development status of vocational education teachers in China, and there are relatively many specific empirical studies.

3.1.3 Research on Professional Development of Vocational Education Teachers

Teacher professional development has two meanings: from the perspective of group, it refers to the process of teachers obtaining professional status, including the systematization of educational knowledge and skills, the professionalization of teacher education and the institutionalization of teacher qualification. From the perspective of individuals, it refers to the process of continuous renewal, evolution and enrichment of teachers' internal professional accomplishment, including teachers' professional knowledge, professional skills, professional emotions, etc. Pre-service education, induction training and in-service training are the main approaches to teacher professional development. Therefore, the research scope of teacher professional development in vocational education mainly includes teacher professional quality and ability, teacher qualification, teacher education, team professionalization, etc. In the research on professional quality and ability of vocational education teachers, Zhong and Li (2019) used grounded theory to conduct coding analysis of China's vocational education teacher policy texts since 1993. It is found that the requirements for teachers' professional accomplishment in the policy text focus on six aspects: teacher ethics and professional ideas, theoretical knowledge, practical knowledge, basic teaching ability, practical teaching ability and professional development ability. The research on teacher qualification in vocational education focuses on the introduction of the foreign vocational education teacher qualification system, while the research on the domestic vocational education teacher qualification system is relatively few. The research on teacher education in the field of vocational education not only explores the training mechanism of Chinese vocational education teachers, but also makes a comparative study of Chinese and foreign vocational education teacher education. The research on professional development of vocational education teachers covers a wide range of contents, including not only the individual professional development of teachers, but also the overall professional development of vocational education teachers. In the field of the study, researchers mostly with international perspective to analysis and thinking, with the method of comparative study on analysis of Chinese and foreign in vocational education teacher professionalism, the differences between the teachers' qualification, personnel training, etc., for reference of foreign vocational education developed countries such as America, Germany's experience, suggestions on vocational education teachers' professional development in our country. According to the literature collected on CNKI, so far researchers' research on vocational education teachers mainly focusses on three aspects: vocational education teacher policy, "double-qualified" teachers and teacher professional development. Among them, for the research of the "double division type" relevant content has always been a hotspot of research on vocational education teachers, from the understanding of the "double division type" to the construction of "double type" teachers, to the new era under the quality and ability of the vocational education teachers need to explore, the researchers understanding of the orientation of vocational education teachers change over time. In terms of research methods, the research on vocational education teachers focuses on theoretical research, with few empirical studies. It mainly relies on a certain vocational education school or a certain region to explore the existing problems and improvement measures of vocational education teachers through a variety of research methods. From the research results of vocational education teachers, the problems of vocational education teachers in the development process of China's vocational education are homogeneous in time and region, focusing on teacher composition structure, teacher professionalism and other issues. Therefore, in the current era of vigorously promoting vocational education, how to solve these problems needs more in-depth thinking (Gong, 2012; Li, 2014; Shi et al., 2021; Wang et al., 2021; Yao, 2002).

3.2 Data Analysis of the Teachers' Resources Allocation in China's Vocational Education

3.2.1 Changes of Faculty and Staff

From the perspective of data over the years, higher vocational (junior college) college teaching and administrative staff can mainly be interpreted from the number and structure of two aspects. In terms of quantity, the number of full-time teachers has shown an increasing trend in the past 10 years, indicating that the higher vocational teachers in China have been developing and expanding continuously in the past 10 years. However, the ratio of full-time teachers to students changed little and remained at 1:23 in the past 10 years, which was still far behind the national standard ratio of 1:18. The number of personnel in research institutions has been shrinking in the past decade, with a 42.35% decrease from 2010 to 2019. In terms of structure, the proportion of full-time teachers in the teaching and administrative staff of the main school has increased year by year, indicating that the teaching and administrative structure of higher vocational colleges in China is being adjusted to streamline administrative, teaching, and auxiliary staff and increase the proportion of full-time teachers (See Table 3.1).

Table 3.1 Change table of staff situation in higher vocational colleges (junior college) from 2010 to 2019

Year	Teacher	School-based staff	Percentage of full-time teachers (%)	Ratio of full-time teachers to students	Personnel of scientific research institutions
2010	404,098	587,171	68.82	1: 23.91	1419
2011	412,624	598,522	68.94	1: 23.24	1494
2012	423,381	607,212	69.73	1: 22.77	1386
2013	436,561	615,993	70.87	1: 22.30	1340
2014	438,300	611,502	71.68	1: 22.97	1169
2015	454,576	625,881	72.63	1: 23.07	1278
2016	466,934	639,656	73.00	1: 23.19	1160
2017	482,070	657,930	73.27	1: 22.92	1056
2018	497,682	674,567	73.78	1: 22.78	984
2019	514,436	688,492	74.72	1: 24.90	818
growth (%)	+27.30	+17.26	–	–	−42.35

*Percentage of full-time teachers refers to the percentage of full-time teachers among the faculty and staff of the main school. In addition to full-time teachers, the staff of the school also includes administrative teachers, auxiliary teaching teachers and working teachers, but does not include the staff of scientific research institutions

As can be seen from the data, the number of both full-time teachers and external teachers has achieved a sharp increase in the past 10 years. Among them, the number of full-time double-qualified teachers in professional courses increased from 167,902 in 2010 to 376,473 in 2019, an increase of 124.22% in 10 years. The employment of double-qualified teachers for professional courses has increased by 88.26% in the past 10 years. China's efforts to build a team of double-qualified teachers have achieved significant results. The proportion of double-qualified teachers among full-time teachers surpassed that of double-qualified teachers hired from outside the university after 2013, indicating that universities gradually pay more attention to the construction of double-qualified teachers for full-time professional courses. From the perspective of the proportion of teachers of specialized courses, teachers of specialized courses account for most external teachers, indicating that universities pay more attention to professional ability when recruiting external teachers (See Table 3.2).

Among the full-time teachers in higher vocational colleges, the number of seniors, associate senior, intermediate and undetermined teachers showed a trend of increasing year by year during the decade, while the number of junior teachers showed a trend of decreasing year by year. In terms of proportion, senior and associate senior titles increased slightly, while intermediate titles increased significantly. These three types of titles are basically stable at 5, 25 and 40% at present. The proportion of junior professional titles is declining year by year, and continues to

Table 3.2 Post classification of teachers in colleges and universities from 2010 to 2019

Year	Full-time teachers are divided according to teaching content			Hire outside teachers according to the teaching content		
	Public course basic course	Professional course		Public course	Professional course	
		In total	Double teacher		In total	Double teacher
2010	359,420	948,907	167,902	71,304	276,830	50,451
2011	368,859	982,462	187,493	75,046	297,638	57,842
2012	379,772	1,016,818	200,013	77,193	310,480	64,332
2013	389,051	1,057,322	211,891	78,017	325,313	65,645
2014	387,024	1,093,283	234,433	79,222	344,789	70,663
2015	390,983	1,123,753	258,042	80,671	365,182	74,764
2016	384,664	1,155,185	283,063	78,007	387,333	85,537
2017	373,325	1,192,017	321,333	80,596	406,798	92,142
2018	380,772	1,215,224	350,881	82,125	423,056	94,857
2019	390,268	1,264,484	376,473	83,956	447,162	94,978
growth (%)	+8.58	+33.26	+124.22	+17.74	+61.53	+88.26

Data source Official website of the Ministry of Education of the People's Republic of China - Literature - Educational Statistics - Educational qualifications of full-time teachers and external teachers in secondary vocational Schools (institutions) (total) (as of 2021.8.8) http://www.moe.gov.cn/s78/A03/moe_560/jytjsj_2019/qg/202006/t20200611_464853.html

Table 3.3 Changes in the number of professional titles of teachers in higher vocational colleges (junior colleges) from 2010 to 2019

Year	Senior	Deputy high	Middle	primary	In rank
2010	14,655	101,133	147,332	105,691	35,287
2011	15,599	103,523	157,529	101,714	34,259
2012	16,933	106,120	166,527	98,865	34,936
2013	18,276	109,543	174,894	96,425	37,423
2014	18,638	110,050	179,358	92,325	37,929
2015	19,816	114,589	186,109	92,168	41,894
2016	20,502	117,170	190,446	92,080	46,736
2017	21,731	123,247	194,635	91,608	50,849
2018	23,113	127,571	199,801	92,767	54,430
2019	24,065	131,051	205,414	94,355	59,551
Growth (%)	+64.21	+29.58	+39.42	−10.73	+68.76

Data source Official website of the Ministry of Education of the People's Republic of China - Literature - Educational Statistics - Educational qualifications of full-time teachers and external teachers in secondary vocational Schools (institutions) (total) (as of 2021.8.8). http://www.moe.gov.cn/s78/A03/moe_560/jytjsj_2019/qg/202006/t20200611_464853.html

decline, and is about 18% at present. The proportion of undetermined ranks has been increasing year by year and shows a trend of continued growth and is now around 12% (See Table 3.3).

As can be seen from Table 3.4, the educational structure of full-time teachers in colleges and universities has undergone great changes in the past 10 years. In terms of quantity, the number of teachers with doctor's degree has increased by 137.49%, the number of teachers with master's degree has increased by + 38.09%, the number of teachers with bachelor's degree has decreased and the number of teachers with junior college or below has decreased significantly. In terms of proportion, nearly half of them had bachelor's degrees in 2010, but by 2019, the proportion had dropped to 35%, with master's degrees making up the largest part. In the past 10 years, the number of full-time teachers with master's and doctoral degrees in Chinese universities has increased significantly, and the educational structure has been significantly optimized.

In terms of the number of secondary vocational school staff and full-time teachers showed a declining trend in the past 10 years, but a turning point appeared in 2018–2019, with a slight increase in the number. The proportion of full-time teachers shows a trend of increasing year by year, which means that secondary vocational schools in the past 10 years to strengthen the reduction of non full-time teachers. The ratio of full-time teachers to students has changed significantly from 1: 24.74 in 2010 to 1: 17.52 in 2019. The ratio is gradually improving (See Table 3.5).

Table 3.4 Change of academic qualifications of full-time teachers in colleges and universities from 2010 to 2019

Year	Doctor	Master	Bachler	Junior college and below
2010	200,337	463,401	656,991	22,398
2011	227,400	488,373	655,118	21,785
2012	254,399	513,793	651,623	20,477
2013	285,353	535,784	654,660	21,068
2014	313,136	552,854	648,230	20,290
2015	338,442	569,321	645,068	19,734
2016	366,289	581,615	634,501	19,563
2017	397,974	596,302	621,137	17,835
2018	433,807	612,308	611,594	15,044
2019	475,787	639,922	610,369	14,067
Growth (%)	+137.49	+38.09	−7.10	−37.20

Data source Official website of the Ministry of Education of the People's Republic of China - Literature - Educational Statistics - Educational qualifications of full-time teachers and external teachers in secondary vocational Schools (institutions) (total) (as of 2021.8.8). http://www.moe.gov.cn/s78/A03/moe_560/jytjsj_2019/qg/202006/t20200611_464853.html

Table 3.5 Change of teaching staff in secondary vocational schools from 2010 to 2019

Year	Full-time teachers	School-based staff	Percentage of full-time teachers (%)	Ratio of full-time teachers to students
2010	680,954	940,070	72.44	1: 24.74
2011	689,363	931,124	74.04	1: 23.25
2012	684,071	909,012	75.25	1: 21.77
2013	668,754	874,171	76.50	1: 20.14
2014	663,782	857,831	77.38	1: 18.93
2015	652,447	833,140	78.31	1: 18.39
2016	643,143	813,370	79.07	1: 18.03
2017	640,398	804,848	79.57	1: 17.96
2018	635,461	793,977	80.04	1: 17.62
2019	642,197	798,471	80.43	1: 17.52

Data source Official website of the Ministry of Education of the People's Republic of China - Literature - Educational Statistics - Educational qualifications of full-time teachers and external teachers in secondary vocational Schools (institutions) (total) (as of 2021.8.8) http://www.moe.gov.cn/s78/A03/moe_560/jytjsj_2019/qg/202006/t20200611_464853.html

3.2.2 The Analysis of Full Time Teachers in Vocational Schools

Overall, the number of full-time teachers in secondary vocational schools showed a decreasing trend in the past 10 years, among which the number of teachers with senior titles decreased by 45.43%, the number of teachers with intermediate titles decreased by 9.98%, the number of teachers with junior titles decreased by 24.01%, and the number of teachers with deputy senior titles increased by 3.79%. In addition, the number of teachers with undecided rank also increased by 33.59%. In terms of proportion, the number of people with intermediate titles has always occupied the largest proportion, which is basically stable at 40%. The proportion of deputy senior and undecided ranks is gradually increasing; The proportion of junior professional titles is decreasing (See Table 3.6).

In the past 10 years, there have been great changes in the educational background of full-time teachers in secondary vocational education. The number of full-time teachers with college degrees, high school degrees or below has decreased significantly, among which the number of teachers with college degrees has decreased sharply from 108,218 to 45,791, a decrease of 57.69%. The number of people with master's degrees increased by 94.03%, from 26,807 to 52,255, while the number of people with bachelor's degrees remained unchanged, while the number of people with doctorate degrees was small and decreased. In the proportion, most of the bachelor's degree, master's degree in the proportion of increasing year by year, junior college degree in the proportion of decreasing year by year. From the situation of higher vocational and secondary vocational teachers in China from 2010 to 2019,

Table 3.6 Professional titles of teachers in secondary vocational schools from 2010 to 2019

Year	Senior	Associate senior	Middle	Primary	In rank
2010	4642	139,673	275,077	201,973	59,589
2011	4927	147,089	278,249	198,996	60,102
2012	4018	153,165	277,495	191,865	57,528
2013	3383	155,455	268,628	182,596	58,692
2014	3179	158,175	266,321	176,856	59,251
2015	2869	157,931	261,890	171,569	58,188
2016	2602	158,549	256,446	165,371	60,175
2017	2552	159,863	252,228	159,561	66,194
2018	2340	156,165	259,817	156,038	70,101
2019	2533	158,939	247,629	153,489	79,607
Growth (%)	−45.43	+13.79	−9.98	−24.01	+33.59

Data source Official website of the Ministry of Education of the People's Republic of China - Literature - Educational Statistics - Educational qualifications of full-time teachers and external teachers in secondary vocational Schools (institutions) (total) (as of 2021.8.8) http://www.moe.gov.cn/s78/A03/moe_560/jytjsj_2019/qg/202006/t20200611_464853.html

on the whole, China's higher vocational teachers are constantly growing, while the secondary vocational teachers are in the process of reducing the total number and adjusting the structure. Among the teachers in higher vocational colleges, the number of full-time teachers is increasing, the proportion of teachers in the main school is increasing year by year, and the number of double-qualified teachers is increasing significantly, but the number of scientific research personnel is decreasing year by year, and the ratio of teachers to students is not significantly improved. In terms of the structure of professional titles, the number of professional titles at all levels has increased significantly except for the junior level. At present, the number of professional titles at all levels has formed a structure proportion of positive senior 5%, deputy senior 25%, intermediate 40%, junior 18% and undecided rank 12%. In terms of educational structure, the number of people with master's degree and master's degree increased significantly, shifting from bachelor's degree to master's degree and master's degree, and constantly evolving toward higher educational structure. Among the teachers in secondary vocational schools, the number of full-time teachers decreases, but the proportion of teachers in the main school increases, and the ratio of teachers to students keeps optimizing. In terms of professional title structure, all levels except deputy senior and undecided rank have been reduced, among which the number of positive seniors has been greatly reduced. At present, the structure of positive senior is less than 1%, deputy senior 25%, middle 40%, junior 24% and undecided rank 12%. In terms of educational structure, the number of people with master's degree has increased significantly, while the number of people with junior college degree, high school degree or below has decreased significantly, forming a structure with bachelor's degree as the main degree and master's degree as the major degree.

From the situation of higher vocational and secondary vocational teachers across the country in 2019, there is a large regional gap in the number of full-time vocational teachers, teacher-student ratio, title structure and educational background structure in China. In terms of number, the number of full-time teachers in eastern and central China is large, while the number of full-time teachers in southwest and northwest China is relatively small. It is worth noting that Jiangsu, Shandong, Henan and Guangdong provinces are very prominent in the number of full-time teachers. In terms of the ratio of teachers to students, 17 provincial administrative regions can meet the standard of 1:18 for higher vocational colleges, and 15 provincial administrative regions can meet the standard of 1:16 for secondary vocational schools. Among them, the ratio of full-time teachers to students in higher vocational and secondary vocational schools in Beijing is about 1:8, far ahead of other regions in China. In terms of title structure, Jiangsu, Shandong, Henan, Guangdong and Hebei lead, followed by Beijing, Liaoning, Zhejiang, Jiangxi, Hubei, Hunan, Sichuan and Shaanxi. The distribution of educational structure is similar to that of professional title structure (Gong, 2012; Li, 2014; Wang et al., 2021).

3.3 Challenges of the Teachers' Resources Allocation in China's Vocational Education

3.3.1 The Teacher-Student Ratio Is Not up to Standard

The number of teachers is an important index to evaluate the number of teachers at all levels. The teacher–student ratio is a better indicator to measure whether the number of teachers is sufficient. According to the statistics published by the official website of the Ministry of Education, the statistics here is the ratio of full-time teachers to students. The teachers in vocational colleges include basic public course teachers and professional course teachers; The teachers of secondary vocational schools include teachers of basic cultural courses, teachers of specialized courses and teachers of practice guidance courses. Student is a student in school. In higher vocational colleges, the ratio of full-time teachers to students remained at about 1:23 during the decade from 2010 to 2019, among which, the lowest point was 1:23.30 in 2013. In 2019, the current peak was 1:24.90. Throughout the past decade, the ratio of full-time teachers to students in higher vocational colleges in China has basically maintained a stable state, which means that the increase of the number of full-time teachers and students in higher vocational colleges in China is roughly the same, but it has never reached the national standard of 1:18. In secondary vocational schools, the ratio of full-time teachers to students has been gradually declining in the past decade, from 1:24.74 in 2010 to 1:17.52 in 2019. It can be seen that the ratio of teachers to students has improved significantly in the past decade, but there is still a gap between it and the national standard ratio of 1:16. In fact, the number of full-time teachers has been in a roughly declining state over the past decade, and the declining teacher–student ratio has meant that the number of students choosing secondary vocational schools has fallen even faster over the past decade.

3.3.2 Uneven Distribution of Teaching and Administrative Staff at All Levels

In higher vocational colleges, the number of full-time teachers has increased from 404,098 in 2010 to 514,436 in 2019, with an increase of 27.30%. The proportion of full-time teachers is also increasing gradually, and it was 74.72% in 2019. In secondary vocational schools, although the number of full-time teachers is decreasing year by year, their proportion is increasing year by year, reaching 80.43% by 2019. However, in accordance with the Notice of Ministry of Personnel and Education on Printing and Distributing The Three Guiding Opinions on Post Establishment and Management of Institutions of Higher Learning, Compulsory Education, Secondary Vocational Schools and Other Educational Institutions (Issued by Ministry of Chinese

People [2007] No. 59) in 2007, The proportion of teachers' posts in secondary vocational schools in the total school posts is generally not less than 85%, There is still a gap between the principle of no more than 15% for other positions. In addition, vocational schools aim to cultivate skilled talents with high quality, so it is inevitable that there is a large demand for practice instructors. However, according to the statistical data of the Ministry of Education, among the 642,197 full-time teachers in China's secondary vocational schools in 2019, there were only 24,180 practice instructors, accounting for less than 4%, which is extremely scarce (Cao, 2021; Shi et al., 2021; Yao, 2002; Zhong & Li, 2019).

3.3.3 The Structure of Vocational Education Teachers' Academic Qualifications

China's vocational education teachers have made great progress in the structure of educational background after long-term construction and development. In terms of number, the number of teachers with doctoral degrees in higher vocational colleges has been increasing by 137.49% from 200,000,337 in 2010 to 475,787 in 2019. The number of teachers with master's degrees in secondary vocational schools is also on the rise, rising 94.03% from 26,807 in 2010 to 52,255 in 2019. In terms of proportion, the proportion of teachers with doctor's degree and master's degree in higher vocational colleges is increasing, while the proportion of teachers with bachelor's degree and below is decreasing. By 2019, the proportion of teachers with doctor's degree is 36.77%. Secondary vocational schools, nearly 10 years of undergraduate course of basic education teachers remain above 80%, and in 2019 reached 84.41%, and in accordance with the requirements, the teachers in higher vocational colleges should have PhD degree and in secondary vocational school teachers should have a master's degree, which means China's vocational education teacher qualifications structure still exists in the condition of teachers' degree is low, It is necessary to improve the structure of teacher education continuously.

3.3.4 The Number of Vocational Education Teachers and Their Academic Qualifications Is Not Evenly Distributed Among Regions

China's vast territory, various provinces and cities from different social political and economic development, vocational education as an integral part of social life, also is closely related to economic conditions, presents the uneven regional development, relatively speaking, vocational education teachers and central region situation is good, in the western region is relatively backward. According to 2019 data: In terms of the number of teachers, the ratio of full-time teachers to students in vocational colleges in the eastern and central regions is relatively good. The average ratio of full-time teachers to students in regular colleges is 1:16.15, and that in secondary vocational schools is 1:17.78. Among them, Beijing ranks first among all the provinces in China, with the ratio of full-time teachers to students being 1:8.36 in universities and 1:8.20 in secondary vocational schools. For example, Tibet has only 1,784 teachers in secondary vocational schools and 2,610 teachers in regular colleges and universities, Qinghai has 2,363 teachers in secondary vocational schools and 4,767 teachers in regular colleges and universities, and Ningxia has 3,063 teachers in secondary vocational schools and 8,422 teachers in regular colleges and universities.

From the perspective of teachers' educational background, teachers in the eastern and central regions have relatively high educational background, while teachers in the western regions have relatively low educational background. This is the case in higher vocational schools, and the gap in the educational background of teachers in secondary vocational schools is more obvious. Among ordinary university teachers, there are 47,882 in Beijing, 44,539 in Jiangsu, 6,647 in Yunnan and 342 in Xizang. Among the teachers in secondary vocational schools, there are few teachers from Tibet and Ningxia without a doctor's degree, and few teachers with a master's degree. Therefore, we should strengthen the regional vocational education teachers' quantity, quality, provincial administrative region on the unbalanced current situation of the development of attention, especially the vocational education teachers in backward area, there was a terrible shortage of several provincial administrative region, narrow the gap in everywhere, promote the development of the vocational education fair, give play to the role of vocational education for the promotion of social economy (Cao, 2021; Shi et al., 2021; Zhong & Li, 2019).

3.3.5 The Quantity and Quality of Teachers

The first dilemma faced by "double-qualified" teachers is the shortage of them. According to statistics released on the official website of the Ministry of Education, in 2019, among full-time teachers of specialized courses in Chinese universities, double-qualified teachers accounted for 29.77%. Among the teachers hired for specialized courses outside school, "double-qualified" teachers accounted for 21.24%. These data, to some extent, reflect the shortage of "double-qualified" teachers in higher vocational colleges in China. Affected by the policy bottleneck, it is difficult to hire enterprise technicians or senior technical business backbone personnel with solid professional theoretical knowledge and rich practical skills. There is a serious shortage of "double-qualified" teachers who can not only carry out theoretical teaching but also guide the operation of skills. Teacher education is the key link of cultivating teachers and the source of improving teachers' professional quality. Besides pre-service training, post-service training is an important way to promote the professional development of "double-qualified" teachers. Rapidly changing times, professional technology is also changing, as the "double division type" teacher, you need to implement lifelong learning to improve personal professional qualities, but from the research situation, although every year there are all kinds of training at all levels, but really have a chance to attend training of teachers is very limited, and even some teachers long-serving had never taken part in training; Most of the training is short term, the time is short, it is difficult to carry out in-depth, the lack of long-term, macroscopic training planning; During the training period, teachers still undertake heavy teaching tasks, and the pressure of both work and training is great. The training method is single, the theory training mainly, the practice opportunity is few; School–enterprise cooperation is not close, enterprises do not want to arrange teachers to the real production position training, but the practice of the post to see; Training effect is not obvious, the training assessment is too formalized, did not play a real role of supervision and guidance. The nature of vocational education determines the nature of the teachers in vocational education. The training of front-line skilled and application-oriented talents in vocational education needs a team of double-qualified teachers, and teacher qualification is the premise and basis to ensure the construction of double-qualified teachers in vocational education. The Outline of The National Medium—and Long-term Plan for Education Reform and Development (2010–2020) clearly states: "Improve the teacher qualification standards that meet the characteristics of vocational education". For a long time, the admittance of teachers in secondary vocational schools only requires educational background, without professional requirements. Normal students in normal colleges have high school education before entering, while normal students in vocational and technical normal colleges have almost zero professional basis before entering, so they must have professional requirements. At present, our country has established the primary and secondary school teacher qualification examination standards, the implementation of the "national standard, provincial examination, county management, school recruitment" management system; But average middle and primary school and secondary vocational school size itself is not as good as professional as many as 367 varieties, even calculate by professional categories, 18, has fewer plus some major recruit, countries have not yet been introduced to vocational school teachers' qualifications examination standard, vocational school teachers' qualification examinations also used the written part of the content in the secondary school. In the future, in order to vigorously develop vocational education and implement the requirement of "two kinds of education are equally important", it is necessary to further explore the standards of secondary vocational schoolteacher qualification examination, which should also highlight the requirements of double teacher quality and pay more attention to the investigation of practical skills besides the teaching ability of teachers.

3.3.6 Job Benefits and Security

From the point of view of social ideas, our traditional notion of liberal arts, skills, and it is widely held vocational education inferior social psychology, thought to be "back to education of choice", in such a social background, the vocational education "double type" teachers cannot get the attention of the society, occupational prestige also impossible. From the perspective of financial input, the state's financial input to application-oriented colleges and universities is lower than that of other types of colleges and universities, which makes the training, scientific research and practice funds of application-oriented colleges and universities unable to be guaranteed, which is also part of the reason for the poor salary of "double-qualified" teachers.

From the perspective of teacher management, vocational colleges have not yet formed a set of scientific and reasonable "double-qualified" teacher team management system. Management mode and its management in colleges and universities by inertia influence, education, skills, theory, practice, scientific research, application, ignoring the characteristics of vocational education, the teacher introduce, title determination, promotion and selection recommendation, etc., ignoring the particularity of "double type" teachers, the "double type" teachers and "the double teacher" one size fits all. There is no long-term management mechanism conducive to "double-qualified" teachers, which leads to the serious loss of talents and the lack of self-development consciousness of "double-qualified" teachers (Cao, 2021; Gong, 2012; Li, 2014; Shi et al., 2021; Wang et al., 2021; Yao, 2002; Zhong & Li, 2019).

3.4 Suggestions on Allocation of Teachers' Resources in China's Vocational Education

3.4.1 Build a Team of Quality Teachers

High-quality vocational education is inseparable from high-quality teachers. For the current vocational education teachers, the total number is insufficient, and the professional quality of teachers needs to be improved. Therefore, how to attract talents into the vocational education teachers needs to be paid attention to. Yang Yongming proposed to establish a salary incentive mechanism to increase the sense of security of teachers in vocational education and promote the stable development of teachers, to attract more talents to join. But salary incentive for forming a high-quality vocational education teacher is not enough, outside strengthen teachers still need to consider the structure of teachers, optimize the structure of the existing vocational education teachers, to solve the present vocational education teachers have a relatively low level of education, the practice ability is weak, also need to make the existing each use for different types of vocational education teachers, Build a team of teachers. In January 2019, The State Council pointed out in the National Vocational Education Reform Implementation Plan that "exploring the establishment of high-level, structured teacher teaching innovation team, teachers' division of labor and cooperation for modular teaching". This marks that the construction of teachers' teaching innovation team in vocational education has been put on the agenda formally and points out the direction for the teaching of teachers' team in vocational education in China. In pedagogy, professional learning community is a common learning organization with sharing (resources, technology, experience, value, etc.) and cooperation as the core, and a common vision as the link to connect teachers together and exchange with each other. It can improve the ability of teachers to solve practical problems, enhance the collaboration and information exchange among members. Enable individuals to benefit from team interactions and develop the ability of individuals to collaborate effectively with others. The teaching innovation team of vocational education teachers can also be regarded as a professional learning community. This new type of teacher team and corresponding teaching method put forward higher requirements on members' education and training ability, practice, and innovation ability, and can also promote team teachers to change the traditional teaching method of subject. The reform of modular teaching mode of professional ability such as "inquiry" and "anchoring" should be carried out to give full play to the main role of students and the leading role of teachers, pay attention to the cultivation of students' ability to solve practical problems, and improve the ability of vocational education to cultivate composite technical skills talents.

3.4.2   Expand Channels for Teacher Training

The training of vocational education teachers is of great significance for improving teachers' comprehensive ability, promoting teachers' professional development, and optimizing the structure of teachers' team. It not only includes teachers' pre-service training education, but also includes teachers' lifelong education. How to carry out practical and effective training for vocational education teachers can consider broadening the channels of teacher training. Combined with the current situation and challenges faced by teacher training in vocational education, the training of teachers can be roughly divided into three parts: colleges, enterprises and foreign countries, among which, the strength of enterprises should be properly used and vigorously developed. For vocational and technical normal colleges, the cultivation of talents should be close to "double-qualified" teachers, and the training scheme and teaching system should be designed with equal emphasis on theory and practice. For in-service teachers, colleges and universities should fully integrate internal resources, play to full-time teachers and part-time teachers and their respective advantages to consider Zhanjiang teachers combination, form support relations, the common preparation, teaching, carry out professional construction, curriculum construction and scientific research, etc., make up the lack of professional teachers' practical experience and the shortage of part-time teachers' education teaching experience, improve the lesson preparation, teaching ability, enhance the teaching effect.

3.4.3 School–Enterprise Cooperation

Since 2019, in principle, teachers of related majors in vocational colleges and application-oriented undergraduate universities should be recruited from those who have more than 3 years working experience in enterprises and have higher vocational education, except for graduates who hold vocational skill level certificates in related fields. Starting from 2020, except for "double-qualified" vocational and technical teachers' majors, it will no longer recruit fresh graduates who have never worked in enterprises for more than three years, and the educational requirements for special high-skilled talents can be appropriately relaxed. According to the documents issued by the Ministry of Education and other departments, the importance of teachers' practical ability in vocational education in China is self-evident, and the acquisition of teachers' practical ability is closely related to enterprises. On the one hand, the practice of colleges and enterprises to build deep cooperation platform, colleges and universities combined with the actual situation make them time plan of the enterprise, for teachers in enterprise training exercise, for teachers to participate in the field practice, not only need to set up inspection standard, but also want to arrange work tasks and salary treatment, from teacher's trouble back at home. On the other hand, vocational education teachers are encouraged to enter cooperative enterprises with scientific research tasks and topics, carry out technical research and development innovation with enterprises in the form of team, and participate in the actual production of enterprises in the way of task-oriented, university–enterprise integration, faculty co-employment and equipment sharing. This way can not only promote teachers to understand the latest industry trends and production research and development technology, but also to achieve their own quality and skills improvement; It is also conducive to economic benefits, so that enterprises can enjoy the talent "dividend", so as to mobilize the enthusiasm of enterprises to participate in vocational education teacher training, and make the two sides carry out in-depth cooperation (Cao, 2021; Gong, 2012; Li, 2014; Shi et al., 2021; Wang et al., 2021; Yao, 2002; Zhong & Li, 2019).

3.4.4 Overseas Study

It is beneficial for vocational education teachers to take part in overseas study to broaden their professional horizons and develop their professional abilities. Colleges and universities can set up special funds for teacher training, select and send outstanding teachers to countries with developed vocational education every year to receive long-term training for more than three months, give priority to front-line teachers, and promote teachers to carry out teaching reform from bottom to top. Through overseas training, teachers can learn the world's cutting-edge vocational education concepts and teaching modes, update their ideas, broaden their horizons, and catch up with the world trend, so as to form a team of teachers with an international vision. First, there is a social cognitive bias toward vocational education, which is associated with the cognitive bias toward vocational education teachers. To change this social concept, the government needs to formulate relevant policies to promote the development of applied colleges and secondary vocational schools, which are currently in a weak position, and correct the public's wrong views on vocational education. Secondly, teachers' professional practice cannot be separated from a good policy environment. In foreign countries, most of the new teachers in vocational schools come from those who have practical experience in enterprises, while in China, most of the vocational teachers come directly from schools due to the institutional and institutional obstacles for enterprise personnel to enter vocational schools. To solve the problem of insufficient practical ability of vocational education teachers in China, the state has issued a series of policies, such as "double-qualified" teachers and the practice of teachers in enterprises, to promote teachers to strengthen professional practice activities and improve teachers' professional practical ability. But the effect of the policies is not obvious. Because the main role of enterprises in vocational education has not been implemented, the vocational education of enterprises is absent, and school–enterprise cooperation is often superficial. Therefore, it is necessary to formulate and implement relevant policies for enterprises as important school-running subjects. Only when enterprises have training institutions and personnel, and school–enterprise cooperation has a foundation or platform can both sides achieve effective, in-depth and practical communication and cooperation on the basis of common interests. Third, deepen the reform of vocational education teachers' personnel system, including teachers' employment, salary and professional title evaluation, so as to create good conditions for the development of vocational education teachers. We will improve the admission system of vocational education teachers, change the previous employment system of application-oriented colleges and universities, and formulate unified standards for colleges and universities to implement. In terms of treatment, it is necessary to strengthen the guarantee of funds for professional development of vocational education teachers. The competent department of education should set up special funds for teacher training, scientific research and other activities in vocational schools, and implement unified management. Make clear the standard of subsidy for vocational education teachers during their further study and post, so as to protect their interests. According to statistics on the official website of the Ministry of Education, the number of senior teachers in secondary vocational schools across the country decreased by 45.43% from 2010 to 2019, and in 2019, the number of senior teachers accounted for only 0.39% of all teachers with professional titles. Teachers in secondary vocational schools belong to professional education like those in higher vocational colleges. If the senior job evaluation system of teachers is not implemented in place, the incentive mechanism of teacher professional development will be greatly reduced, which will easily lead to job burnout and is not conducive to the development of teachers. In the teaching process, we should give full play to the leading role of teachers with professional skills and practical experience, so that they can guide and help teachers with less practical experience. It is important to note that although this part of the teachers' practical application ability is stronger, the lack of related education teaching experience and knowledge reserve tend to lack the corresponding teaching experience and teaching skills, teaching theoretical level remains to be promoted, therefore, to increase the relevant content of the training for this kind of teacher education teaching, improve the teaching quality. Practical teachers and theoretical teachers help each other to realize the transformation of "double-qualified" teachers. In terms of teacher employment, we should perfect the admittance system of "double-qualified" teachers and broaden the channels of introducing "double-qualified" teachers. For the "double type" teachers and reserve force, should consider setting more accurate, more in line with the actual situation of faculty recruitment standards, for example, allows technology outstanding business but no certificate to test the recruitment of teachers, and admitted to conform to the requirements of the personnel in the implementation of teaching as a part-time, but must be on the obtainment of high standard, strict, must wait for the corresponding teacher qualification certificate to be given to the full. In terms of salary, we should ensure the financial investment of the state to the "double-qualified" teachers and set up special funds for the training and scientific research of the "double-qualified" teachers. Since the work of "double-qualified" teachers is often more onerous than that of ordinary teachers, it can be considered to set up an independent salary incentive mechanism for "double-qualified" teachers in combination with the actual situation. In terms of professional title evaluation, all localities should, under the principle of "controlling the total amount and delegating power at the micro level", implement flexible management of vocational school teachers and expand the schools' rights of personnel management and autonomy of internal distribution. Because of "double type" teachers in such aspects as source, work content and the general teachers, should be considered on the policy of "double type" teachers to tilt, or set up separate title assess channel and standards, ensure that in the title "double type" teachers' evaluation on a fixed proportion, as well as encourage more outstanding professionals to "double type" teachers (Cao, 2021; Gong, 2012; Li, 2014; Shi et al., 2021; Wang et al., 2021; Yao, 2002; Zhong & Li, 2019).

References

Cao, Y. (2021). The review of the 13th five-year plan and the prospect of the 14th five-year plan for the construction of vocational education teachers. *China Vocational and Technical Education, 20*(10), 11–17.

Gong, X. (2012). Research on teacher policy of vocational education in China since the reform and opening up. *China Vocational and Technical Education, 4*(21), 26–32.

Li, S. (2014). The orientation of teacher professional development in vocational education from the evolution of the "double-qualified" teacher policy. *Teacher Education Research, 26*(3), 17–22.

Shi, X., Fu, C., & Li, X. (2021). From "double teachers" to "three teachers": A study on the turning of teacher development in vocational education in the new era. *Research in Vocational Education, 20*(2), 74–79.

Wang, F., Luo, X., & Wu, J. (2021). Review and reflection on professional development policies of vocational education teachers in China since the reform and opening up. *Vocational Education Research, 22*(2), 4–10.

Yang, Y., Liu, X., Huang, F., Zhao, C., & Li, J. (2021). Research on innovative training of secondary vocational education teachers under 1+X certificate system. *Research in Vocational Education, 20*(6), 4–9.

Yao, G. (2002). Interpretation of "double-qualified" teachers in vocational education. *China Vocational and Technical Education, 20*(6), 30–31.

Zhong, J., & Li, Y. (2019). Research on teacher professionalism in vocational education: An analysis of teacher policy in vocational education based on grounded theory. *Vocational and Technical Education, 40*(25), 29–34.

Chapter 4
China's Vocational Education Financial Mechanism System

This chapter explores China's vocational educational financial mechanism system. Vocational education is an important part of China's education, for China's economic and social development, personnel training to make an important contribution. This study analyzes the current characteristics of vocational education finance based on the data of China's Statistical Yearbook of Education Funding from 2010 to 2018 and finds that there are problems such as insufficient total funding for vocational education, regional imbalance and low level of funding per student, and puts forward some suggestions to solve these problems. Vocational education is an important part of China's education and an important way to promote economic and social development and employment. Finance of vocational education plays an important role in the development of vocational education, especially in the material security and resource allocation of vocational education. Since the reform and opening, China has carried out corresponding vocational education financial policy reform in different stages according to the national conditions, and constantly improved the financial mechanism and system of vocational education, to give full play to the role of vocational education finance and promote the development of vocational education.

4.1 Literature Review

The financial problem of vocational education is one of the important problems in vocational education research. Finance plays an important role in promoting the development of vocational education. Reviewing the domestic research, the research on vocational education in China is relatively rich, while the research on vocational education finance has gradually become rich in the twenty-first century, mainly involving the following aspects.

© The Author(s), under exclusive license to Springer Nature Singapore Pte Ltd. 2022
E. Xue and J. Li, *China's Vocational Education Reform*, Exploring Education
Policy in a Globalized World: Concepts, Contexts, and Practices,
https://doi.org/10.1007/978-981-19-0748-7_4

4.1.1 Research on the Financial System of Vocational Education

The research on the financial system of vocational education is one of the key points in the research on the financial system of vocational education. Yuan and He (2019) in the forty years review and evaluation of China's education finance reform "mentioned in the education subject to the education system and financial system, financial system construction in education funding system, government spending on education between share system, education funding system and financial management system of education financial system analysis framework, The change and present situation of education finance system are studied. In The Current Situation and Problems of the Financial System of Secondary Vocational Education, Fang (2007) believes that the financial system of vocational education in China has been continuously reformed and steadily promoted since the founding of the People's Republic of China and actively explored the establishment of a financial system of vocational education with Chinese characteristics. Hu (2020) believes that China's vocational education has not yet formed a financial system that meets its own development needs and is different from ordinary education in Research on Fiscal Policy of Vocational Education in China: Review, Sorting out and Prospect. Educational investment is the material basis of educational development, and educational investment system is an important part of educational financial system. Zhang (2011) found in his Research on Financial Policies for The Development of Vocational Higher Education that China's fiscal and tax policies related to higher vocational education finance are not systematic, and there are no special laws and regulations to serve higher vocational education as the main target. Nian and Pan (2019) in The Comparison and Enlightenment of The Financing Mechanisms of Vocational Education in the United States, Germany and Japan, through comparative analysis of the financing mechanisms of the United States, Germany and Japan, proposed that China's vocational education needs to build a perfect legal system to ensure adequate funding input. China's vocational education allocates educational funds according to administrative subordination. The funds of vocational high schools are allocated by the competent educational administrative departments, the funds of technical schools are mainly invested by state-owned enterprises, and the funds of higher vocational schools oversee the educational administrative departments. The funding sources of vocational education mainly include five categories: national financial education funds, sponsors' input in private schools, social donations, enterprise income and other education funds. State financial funds and business income are the main sources of funds for secondary vocational education and higher vocational education.

4.1.2 Research on the Expenditure Mechanism of Vocational Education Funds

The expenditure mechanism of vocational education funds affects the development of vocational education. Zhu (2014) found in The Guarantee of Funds for Vocational Education under the Background of Fiscal and Tax System Reform that the proportion of financial funds for vocational education in the total financial expenditure was the lowest among all types and levels of education during 2005–2012. The proportion of expenditure of secondary vocational education in the total expenditure of education is higher than that of higher vocational education. Zhang (2010) in the analyzing the current situation of China's secondary vocational education funds and related thinking, points out that China's education funds expenditure in the long term there is a problem of the unreasonable proportion of investment: investment overall tilt to higher education, and in the secondary education to the ordinary high school education, lead to secondary vocational education investment ratio is too low.

4.1.3 Research on Education Finance Based on the Comparison Between Vocational Education and General Education

There are some differences in education finance between vocational education and general education in China. In An Analysis of Investment in Higher Vocational Education in China, Li (2012) pointed out the imbalance between the financial investment in higher vocational education and the investment in undergraduate education. Both the number of schools and the number of students enrolled in higher vocational education exceeded that of undergraduate education, and the actual investment was much lower than that of undergraduate education. At present, most of China's higher vocational schools mainly rely on tuition income to maintain daily operation, which is different from foreign higher vocational schools that rely on financial appropriation. Dong (2016) analyzed the financial investment in Higher vocational education in China in The Analysis of National Financial Investment in Higher Vocational Education, and concluded that the national financial investment in higher vocational education was less than that in ordinary undergraduate education at the same stage. Based on this, we should improve the status of vocational education and improve the legislation of vocational education.

4.1.4 Research on the Financial Equity of Vocational Education

The financial equity of vocational education is mainly reflected in the inequity between regions, between urban and rural areas and between schools. Qiu (2011) found in a study on The Financial Equity of Secondary Vocational Education in China—Also on the Policy of Free Secondary Vocational Education and Its Improvement by comparing the per-student expenditure of secondary vocational education from 2002 to 2006 in Shanghai, the economically developed region, Jiangxi and Henan provinces in the central region and Guizhou Province in the western region. Shanghai's total investment in secondary vocational education and the growth rate are much higher than the provinces in the central and western regions. In 2006, Shanghai's education expenditure per student for secondary vocational education was about eight times that of Henan province, seven times that of Guizhou province and six times that of Jiangxi Province, with obvious regional differences. Influenced by China's emphasis on the construction of urban secondary vocational education, the gap between urban and rural secondary vocational education is extremely significant. Shen (2018) found in "Analysis of Differences in Allocation of Vocational Education Funds in recent Ten Years" through statistical analysis of data from 2007 to 2016 that the total education funds per student and the financial education funds per student of secondary and higher vocational education showed a gradient decline from Beijing, Tianjin and Shanghai, the east, the west and the central region, while the central region collapsed. Through the above literature, it can be found that scholars have carried out a large number of extensive studies on the finance of vocational education in four aspects: financial system, expenditure mechanism, financial comparison between vocational education and general education at the same stage, and financial equity of vocational education, and have achieved rich results. From the current research, most scholars have reached the following consensus: China's vocational education financial system and mechanism has not completely separated from the general education, forming an educational administrative system with Chinese characteristics; The expenditure of vocational education in China is small; The financial input of vocational education in China is much lower than that of general education. The finance of vocational education in China is confronted with the problems of fairness between the land range, between urban and rural areas and between schools. Based on the data of China's Statistical Yearbook of Education Funding from 2010 to 2018, this study analyzes the current characteristics of vocational education finance and puts forward some suggestions for the challenges and problems facing it (Dong, 2016; Li, 2012; Nian & Pan, 2019; Qiu, 2011; Shen, 2018; Zhang, 2010, 2011; Zhu, 2014).

4.2 Data Analysis

Since the twenty-first century, China has attached great importance to vocational education, formulated and implemented a series of policies on vocational education, and made great progress in vocational education. The development of vocational education cannot do without the support of funds. The funding of vocational education is the key to the development of vocational education and provides material guarantee for the development of vocational education.

4.2.1 Investment in Vocational Education

The Outline of the National Medium-and Long-term Plan for Education Reform and Development (2010–2020), issued in 2010, clearly calls for the development of vocational education and the improvement of its quality. It can be concluded that from 2010 to 2018, China's educational funds have been increasing continuously from 1,956.185 billion yuan to 4,614.3 billion yuan in 8 years, with a total increase of 135.88%. China has made great efforts to develop education and continuously increased government input. The proportion of government spending on education in China has risen from 74.99% to more than 80% and will remain above 80% for a long time. To some extent, this shows that the country has paid more attention to education. Government spending on education increased by 152.19% from 1.467.07 trillion yuan to 3.699577 trillion yuan. In 2019, government spending on education exceeded 4 trillion yuan for the first time, accounting for 4.04% of GDP. From 2010 to 2018, China's investment in vocational education increased year by year, including an 18% increase in 2011 compared with 2010. The amount spent on vocational education in 2018 nearly doubled from 2010 to 336.724 billion yuan. But on the whole, the proportion of vocational education expenditure in national education expenditure and national financial education expenditure is low and presents a slight downward trend. This shows that vocational education is still relatively inadequate compared with other education under the background of increasing national financial funds for education. Funds for vocational education consist of funds for secondary and higher vocational education. Spending on secondary vocational education has shown an overall trend of growth, rising from 67.894 billion yuan in 2010 to 120.797 billion yuan in 2018. Education funds for vocational high schools and technical schools are constantly expanding. Among them, the funding for vocational high school education increased from 50.930 billion yuan to 86.893 billion yuan, an increase of 70.61%. The funding for technical schools increased from 16.964 billion yuan to 33.904 billion yuan, an increase of 99.86%. Funding for higher vocational education roughly doubled from 2010 to 2018, reaching 215.927 billion yuan in 2018. The investment in higher vocational education is more than that of secondary vocational education.

The funds for vocational education shall consist of the state financial funds for education, the investment of the sponsors of privately run schools, the income from donations, the enterprise income and other educational funds. In terms of secondary vocational education, the state financial funds and enterprise income account for more than 96% of the vocational education funds, while the proportion of sponsors' input, donation income and other educational funds in private schools is very low. The proportion of government expenditure on education in secondary vocational education is increasing steadily, rising to 89% at the highest. In the aspect of higher vocational education, state financial funds and business income are the main components of higher vocational education funds. It is found that the growth rate of national financial expenditure on higher vocational education is higher than that of business income, and gradually becomes the most important source of higher vocational education expenditure. In the past nine years, government spending on education increased from 49.163 billion yuan to 140.994 billion yuan, and business revenue increased from 49.933 billion yuan to 66.661 billion yuan. Therefore, whether it is secondary vocational education or higher vocational education, the state finance is the most important source of educational funds (Dong, 2016; Fang, 2007; Hu, 2020; Li, 2012; Nian & Pan, 2019; Qiu, 2011; Shen, 2018; Yuan & He, 2019; Zhang, 2010, 2011; Zhu, 2014).

4.2.2 The Allocation of Funds for General Education and Vocational Education

Compared with general education, the investment of vocational education in China is low. In terms of secondary vocational education, the investment of general high school education is far greater than that of vocational high school and technical school education. In 2018, 472.465 billion yuan was spent on regular high school education, while only 120.797 billion yuan was spent on secondary vocational education. Secondary vocational education and ordinary high school enrollment scale is roughly the same, the total investment gap between the two is huge. In 2010, China's higher vocational education funds amounted to 105.149 billion yuan, while the general undergraduate education funds reached 444.638 billion yuan. By 2018, China's funding for higher vocational education had increased to 215.927 billion yuan, while that for general undergraduate education had reached 969.949 billion yuan. Higher vocational education and higher general education are about the same in the number of students, and the gap in funding is about four times. The level of vocational education per student is low in China. In 2018, the per student education expenditure of vocational high schools and technical schools was 20,550.31 yuan and 16,918.86 yuan, respectively, while that of regular high schools was 20,406.55 yuan. Higher vocational education is 23,659.41 yuan, which is only half of the education budget per student for higher education. From 2010 to 2018, the per capita funding for secondary and higher vocational education showed an increasing trend. The per capita funding for vocational high schools increased by 1.5 times, technical schools by 78.99%, and higher vocational education by 10,173.49 yuan.

Since the promulgations of the Education Law of the People's Republic of China in 1995, the expenditure of educational facilities and public expenditure per student in the public finance budget have become important indicators to measure the growth of education investment at all levels. The two situations are like the situation of education funding per student. From 2010 to 2018, the education service expense expenditure per student and public expenditure per student in the public finance budget of vocational education showed an overall growth trend, as shown in Tables 3.5 and 3.6. In 2018, the average budgetary expenditure of vocational high schools and technical schools was 15,297.45 yuan and 11,930.99 yuan, 3.3 times and 2.6 times higher than 2010, respectively, with an average annual growth rate of 16.5% and 12.9%, respectively. The average public financial budget for higher vocational education increased from 5,838.87 yuan to 15,461.74 yuan per student, an increase of 1.65 times, with an average annual growth rate of 13.6%. In terms of public expenditure per student, vocational high schools and technical schools were 5,282.82 yuan and 5,260.48 yuan respectively, 4.1 times and 3.1 times the 2010 figures, with an average annual growth rate of 20.7% and 15.5%, respectively. Higher vocational education was 2.8 times that of 2010, with an annual growth rate of 15.7%.

Through horizontal comparison of the educational operation expenses and public expenditure per student in the public financial budget of general education and vocational education at the same level, it is found that the average expenditure of secondary and higher vocational education is still generally low. In terms of education expenditure per student in the public financial budget, vocational high schools are only 390.79 yuan higher than regular high schools, technical schools are 1589.9 yuan lower than regular high schools, and vocational schools are 8,032.08 yuan lower than regular undergraduate schools. No matter for higher education or secondary education, compared with the general education at the same level, the education cost per student of vocational education has always been insufficient in the 8 years of public finance budget and has a trend of further decrease. In terms of public budget expenditure per student, vocational high schools are 1,052.6 yuan higher than regular high schools, technical schools are 849.92 yuan higher than regular high schools, and vocational schools are 3,895.37 yuan lower than regular undergraduate schools. In terms of the growth rate of expenditure per student, the average annual growth rate of education expenditure per student in the public finance budget of ordinary senior high schools and ordinary undergraduate schools was 16.5% and 10.5% respectively, and the average annual growth rate of public expenditure per student in the public finance budget was 18.3% and 10.6% respectively. In contrast, vocational high schools in secondary vocational education saw a similar increase in per pupil expenditure, while technical schools saw a lower increase in per pupil expenditure than regular high schools. The growth rate of expenditure per student in vocational colleges is higher than that of ordinary undergraduate schools. This shows that from 2010 to 2018, the country attaches great importance to the development of vocational education, and there is a trend of inclined to vocational education funding. However, the average cost of vocational education is higher than that of general education, and the average cost of vocational education still needs to be increased (Fang, 2007; Hu, 2020; Li, 2012; Nian & Pan, 2019; Zhang, 2010, 2011; Zhu, 2014).

4.2.3 Regional Investment in Vocational Education

There is a big gap between the provinces in our country and the proportion of the national financial investment in education is different. In 2018, Guangdong spent 441.478 billion yuan on education, ranking first in the country; Ningxia Hui Autonomous Region spent the least on education, with 24.354 billion yuan. The difference in education spending between the two provinces is 417.124 billion yuan. State funds for education in Tibet account for 98.7%, the vast majority of which are state funds for education. The proportion of state finance education in Zhejiang is the lowest in the country, only 73.5%.

There is a big gap in the investment of vocational education among various provinces in China. In 2018, Guangdong spent 34.997 billion yuan on vocational education, the highest among all provinces in China. The Tibet Autonomous Region spent the lowest amount on vocational education in China, 751 million yuan. From the perspective of the proportion of vocational education funds in education funds, Jilin Province has the highest proportion, reaching 11.08%, and Shanghai has the lowest proportion, only 2.93%. Hunan city has the highest proportion of the financial expenditure of vocational education in the state, while Tibet Autonomous Region has the lowest. According to the observation data, there is a prominent regional imbalance in the investment of vocational education in China, which is closely related to the economic and social development level of different regions, the development scale of vocational education and its education policies. There is also a large gap in education expenditure in the public budget of various provinces in China. In 2018, Guangdong spent 19.39 billion yuan from the public budget on vocational education, the highest in the country, including 3.884 billion yuan for vocational high schools, 5.406 billion yuan for technical schools, and 10.1 billion yuan for vocational and technical schools. The Tibet Autonomous Region's public budget spending on education was only 391 million yuan. Except for Ningxia Hui Autonomous Region, Qinghai Province and Tibet Autonomous Region, the other 28 provinces spent an average of 2.206 billion yuan on vocational high schools, 807 million yuan on technical schools, and 4.305 billion yuan on higher vocational schools. On the whole, higher vocational education in China has received more financial support than secondary vocational education, and the financial guarantee is relatively sufficient (Dong, 2016; Li, 2012; Nian & Pan, 2019; Qiu, 2011; Shen, 2018; Zhang, 2010, 2011; Zhu, 2014).

4.3 Challenges of China's Vocational Education Financial Mechanism System

Educational investment is the material basis of educational development. Our country attaches great importance to the development of education, the scale of educational funds is constantly expanding, and the financial input is constantly increasing. From 2010 to 2019, China's education spending increased by 156.51%, with an average annual growth rate of 11.12%. The national spending on education in 2019 was 5.017812 trillion yuan, exceeding the 5 trillion yuan mark for the first time. In 1993, China issued the Outline of Education Reform and Development, which stated that by the end of 2000 the proportion of government spending on education in GDP should reach 4%. Until 2012, China's fiscal spending on education reached 4% of GDP for the first time and remained above 4% until 2019. Government spending on education was 4004.655 billion yuan in 2019, exceeding 4 trillion yuan for the first time. But through the above data analysis we found that China's financial development of vocational education is facing some problems and challenges, mainly for vocational education financial investment insufficiency, the total vocational education funding structure diversification degree is not high, uneven regional vocational education financial investment, the low level of China vocational education funds and vocational education funds investment policy implementation does not reach the designated position in five aspects.

4.3.1 The Total Financial Input in Vocational Education Is Insufficient, and the Proportion of the Total Educational Funds Is Relatively Low

The funding of vocational education is the key to the development of vocational education. With the continuous development of vocational education, the financial investment in vocational education also increases accordingly. From 2010 to 2018, China's funding for vocational education increased from 173.043 billion yuan to 336.724 billion yuan. Although the expenditure of education and vocational education in China is increasing, the proportion of the expenditure of vocational education in the national education is always small. The proportion of vocational education expenditure in the national expenditure is relatively stable, basically maintaining within 7–8.5% from 2010 to 2018. Funds for vocational education increased at an average annual rate of 8.82%. Of the total investment in vocational education, 38% was spent on secondary vocational education and 62% on higher vocational education on average. In terms of the annual growth rate of funding input, secondary vocational education is slightly lower than that of higher vocational education. There is a big gap between vocational education and ordinary high school education and ordinary higher education in China. In 2018, for example, China spent 472.465 billion yuan on the education of regular high schools, accounting for 10.24% of the national education budget; For general undergraduate programs, 969.949 billion yuan, accounting for 21.02%; Vocational high schools and technical schools spent 86.893 billion yuan and 33.904 billion yuan, accounting for 1.88% and 0.73%, respectively. In a word, although the investment in vocational education in China is increasing year by year, it does not account for a high proportion in the whole education expenditure. Compared with general education, the proportion of investment in vocational education in all stages is low (Dong, 2016; Fang, 2007; Hu, 2020; Nian & Pan, 2019; Li, 2012; Qiu, 2011; Shen, 2018; Yuan & He, 2019; Zhang, 2010, 2011; Zhu, 2014).

4.3.2   The Diversification of the Funding Structure of Vocational Education, and the Mechanism of Raising Funds Through Multiple Channels Is Not Perfect

The funds for vocational education are composed of five categories: the state financial funds for education, the sponsors' input in privately run schools, donation income, enterprise income and other educational funds. According to the above data analysis, from 2010 to 2018, the main funding sources of secondary vocational education and higher vocational education were state financial education funds and career income, accounting for about 95% of the total funding of education. In terms of the percentage of career income, the cost of vocational education for students and their families is still relatively high. The national investment in secondary vocational education is significantly greater than that in higher vocational education, which means higher vocational education needs to spend more education costs than secondary vocational education. At the same time, from 2010 to 2018, in the vocational education funds of private schools, the input from sponsors and social donations accounted for a very low proportion of vocational education, less than 1% combined. From 2010 to 2018, the investment structure of vocational education in China has not changed much, and the state financial education funds and career income remain the main part of education funds. This shows that China needs to further promote the diversification of investment structure of vocational education funds. In addition, the high proportion of career income, students and families burden higher education costs which hinders the healthy development of China's vocational education. At present, the composition of the investment in vocational education shows that the funding source of vocational education in China is relatively single, mainly from the financial input and career income, and the enthusiasm of social forces and citizens to participate in running schools has not been fully mobilized, and the channels of increasing the funds of vocational education through multiple channels have not been formed. Therefore, in addition to the state's further investment in secondary and higher vocational education, society and individual citizens also need to share part of the cost of vocational education to promote the coordinated development of secondary and higher vocational education.

4.3.3 Financial Input in Vocational Education Is Not Balanced Among Regions

There is a big gap in economic development between the eastern, central and western regions of China, which affects the development of vocational education to some extent. The eastern region spent an average of 13.836 billion yuan on vocational education. The central region received 11.03 billion yuan; The figure for the western region was 7.142 billion yuan. The investment of vocational education in China is decreasing in the eastern, central and western regions. From the perspective of the proportion of vocational education funds in the total education funds, there is a large gap between provinces and cities. Jilin Province accounted for the highest proportion, reaching 11.08%, and Shanghai the lowest, only 2.93%. There is also a big gap in the proportion of the financial funds of vocational education in the national financial education among provinces and cities, among which the highest is 10.04% in Hunan province and the lowest is 2.84% in Xizang Province. In the vocational education funds, the average proportion of national financial education funds in each province is 75.40%, the highest is 95.74% in Tibet, the lowest is 62.44% in Guangxi. This shows that the national financial funds for vocational education are the most important part of the provincial vocational education funds, but the role of the national financial funds for vocational education is different between the provinces, which is related to the provincial economic development level, the demand for vocational talents, vocational education policies and other factors. There is also a large gap in education expenditure in the general public budget of various provinces in China. According to the above data analysis, although different regions in China have different levels of financial support, overall, higher vocational education has greater financial support than secondary vocational education, and its funding is relatively sufficient. Regional vocational education funds investment imbalance, embrace budget education funding gap is bigger also, this kind of situation will further widen the gap between regional vocational education development, caused the students resource gap between regions, adding to regional economic development imbalance, this conflicts with education fair thought, is not conducive to the construction of a harmonious society (Fang, 2007; Hu, 2020; Qiu, 2011; Shen, 2018; Yuan & He, 2019).

4.3.4 The Level of Funding Per Student for Vocational Education Is Relatively Low, Which Is Not Compatible with the High Cost of Vocational Education

The study of education cost in developed countries shows that the cost of running vocational education is 2.64 times that of ordinary education, that is, the judgment that the cost of developing vocational education is higher is generally accepted. However, the investment of vocational education in China is always lower than that of general education. From 2010 to 2018, the per capita expenditure of vocational education in China showed an increasing trend, but the per capita expenditure of vocational education was still lower than that of general education, especially higher vocational education. Take the data of 2018 as an example, the higher vocational education is 23,659.41 yuan, which is half of the average education expenditure of higher undergraduate students. Education and public expenditure per student in public financial budget are important indicators to measure the growth of expenditure input. Through data analysis, it is found that in the secondary and higher education stage, compared with the general education at the same level, the education cost per student of vocational education in the public finance budget has always been insufficient for 8 years, and shows a further decreasing trend. From the perspective of the growth rate of education expenditure per student, the growth rate of vocational high schools with secondary vocational education is similar, while that of technical schools is lower than that of ordinary high schools. The growth rate of expenditure per student in vocational colleges is higher than that of ordinary undergraduate schools. This shows that from 2010 to 2018, the country attaches great importance to the development of vocational education, and there is a trend that the allocation of education funds is inclined to vocational education funds. However, the average cost of vocational education is much higher than that of general education, and the average cost of vocational education still needs to be increased. The low cost per student of vocational education affects the training of high-quality technical personnel to some extent. At the same time, under the influence of the concept of the supremacy of general education, the average expenditure of vocational education is low, resulting in more burden of education costs for individuals and families, which further reduces the willingness to choose vocational education (Dong, 2016; Li, 2012; Qiu, 2011; Shen, 2018).

4.3.5   The Policy on Investment in Vocational Education Is Not Sound and the Implementation Is Not in Place

The investment of educational funds is the premise of the development of vocational education. The development of vocational education is inseparable from the support and guidance of relevant funds policies and regulations, but at present, the relevant laws and regulations in China on the secondary and higher vocational education funds are mainly directional and principled guidance, not strong pertinently. The standard of expenditure per student is the basic basis of public finance investment in vocational education, and also the basic basis of establishing scientific and reasonable cost-sharing mechanism of vocational education. In 1996, China's Vocational Education Law clearly stipulated that "people's governments of provinces, autonomous regions and municipalities directly under the Central Government shall set standards for the average funding of the number of students in vocational schools in their respective regions". In 2005, the Decision of The State Council on Vigorously Developing Vocational Education clearly stated that "people's governments at all levels should increase their support for vocational education and gradually increase the investment of public finance in vocational education". "And required that" from 2006, the proportion of urban education surcharge arranged for vocational education should not be less than 20% in general areas and not less than 30% in areas where nine-year compulsory education has been universal". The Outline of The National Medium - and Long-term Plan for Education Reform and Development (2010–2020) further defines the responsibilities of governments at all levels and improves the education funding input mechanism at all levels. For example, "Improve the cost-sharing mechanism for non-compulsory education and implement the mechanism for raising funds by the government, industries, enterprises and other social forces in accordance with the law for secondary vocational education". In fact, the progress of implementing these policies in most provinces in China is relatively slow and different, which is related to the different levels of economic development and the focus of education investment in the regions. The inadequacy of the investment policy in vocational education will not only lead to the failure of vocational colleges to meet the needs of social development and the shortage of high-level vocational talents, but also affect the development of some existing vocational colleges, and even affect the normal teaching and the quality of vocational education. Departments issued by the Ministry of Education of the modern vocational education system construction plan (2014–2020) "proposed that by 2020, formed to meet the needs of development, depth fusion, secondary vocational higher education, vocational education and ordinary education to communicate with each other, manifests the lifelong education idea, with Chinese characteristics, the level of modern vocational education system. "Modernization of Education in China 2035", issued in 2019, proposed the development goal of significantly improving the service capacity of vocational education in China, and required to promote the coordinated development of secondary vocational education and regular high school education, pointing out the direction for the development of vocational education (Dong, 2016; Fang, 2007; Hu, 2020; Nian & Pan, 2019; Li, 2012; Qiu, 2011; Shen, 2018; Yuan & He, 2019; Zhang, 2010, 2011; Zhu, 2014).

4.4 Suggestions on China's Vocational Education Financial Mechanism System

4.4.1 Fulfilling Government Duties and Ensuring the Investment in Vocational Education

Educational funds are the important material basis for the development of education in China. In 2012, China achieved the goal of "accounting for 4% of GDP in government spending on education." Until 2019, China maintained the standard that government spending on education accounted for more than 4% of GDP, giving full play to the role of government finance in supporting education. As an important part of education, vocational education aims at cultivating talents with applied skills. The development of vocational education cannot be separated from the funds of vocational education. The cost of cultivating talents varies with different types of education. The average cost of general education is lower than that of vocational education. At present, the investment of vocational education at all levels in China is lower than that of general education, and the financial investment of vocational education is less than that of general education. While the total amount of national education funding increases, we will ensure that the investment in vocational education increases. We will gradually increase the proportion of government investment in vocational education funds to ensure that the government's financial funds for vocational education increase year by year. We will continue to raise the proportion of government investment in vocational education to the international standard of 25%. We will fully implement the rule that no less than 30% of urban education surcharges should be used for vocational education. No less than 30% of new educational resources should be spent on vocational education. In addition, a system of major special investment in vocational education should be established to further enhance the ability of vocational education to serve the economic and social development and the all-round development of human beings through the construction and development of key projects. For example, the funding for the construction of cross-regional and cross-industry practical training bases, the funding for the construction of colleges or majors that are conducive to promoting employment and entrepreneurship, the special subsidy for the cultivation of high-skilled talents needed for the national high-tech development, and the flexible response to emergencies, such as the economic crisis, The financial support is conducive to stimulating demand, increasing employment and ensuring the growth of professional support for skilled personnel training. Set up increasing the responsibility of professional education of the central government fiscal transfer payment system, according to the economic development around the situation, to do a good job of the central government transfer payments, especially in economically backward regions and countries strategic key development area increase the intensity of the central funds transfer payment, to continue and expand all kinds of special construction of vocational education by the central government.

4.4.2 Accelerating the Establishment and Improvement of an Independent Financial Mechanism for Vocational Education

Education is of great importance to the country and the Party. In the new era, it is required to vigorously promote the status of vocational education, accelerate the construction of a modern vocational education system, and meet the demand for diversified talents to support economic and social development. China must timely revise and improve the laws and regulations on the investment of financial funds in vocational education and strengthen the connection and cooperation between relevant laws and regulations. To define and strengthen the corresponding responsibilities and division of labor of the government at all levels in the investment of funds, to form a set of more scientific and perfect national system and policies of the financial investment of vocational education, to further enhance the pertinence of vocational education policies, is conducive to the implementation of policies in accordance with local conditions. China should strive to improve the mechanism of vocational education funding, which is mainly invested by the government and raised by various sectors of society through various channels and build a financial funding guarantee system suitable for the development of modern vocational education system to meet the needs of the construction of modern vocational education system. Based on the public welfare nature of vocational education, the government should play a leading role in ensuring the healthy development of vocational education while playing the role of the market.

4.4.3 Speeding Up the Formulation and Implementation of Standards for Funding Per Student for Vocational Education

According to China's eastern, central and western region's economic and social development level and vocational education training costs, China vocational colleges is put forward by the state funds standard formulation principle, regulate NECs expenditures on the composition of the content, in accordance with the law, promote the provincial government to formulate and implement the vocational colleges embrace China funds basic standards and funding the development of the basic standards work, provide scientific basis for vocational education investment. Higher vocational schools will continue to be included in the financial budgets of regular institutions of higher learning, and gradually achieve the level of budgetary appropriations per student at higher vocational schools reaching and slightly higher than the level of budgetary appropriations per student of regular undergraduate institutions in the region. The budgetary funds per student at secondary vocational schools should not be less than twice the standard of local ordinary high schools. We will ensure a steady increase in expenditure per student and public expenditure per student in vocational colleges, improve their conditions for running schools, strengthen their basic capacity building and create conditions for their sustainable development.

4.4.4 Improving the Mechanism for Raising Funds for Vocational Education in Various Ways

Vocational education provides the skills needed for the development of social economy, directly serves the development of social economy and should maintain a direct and close connection with the society. Encouraging diversified investment by individuals and enterprises will help to strengthen the links between vocational education and industry and make vocational education more career-oriented and reflective. At the same time, the participation of private capital and market forces in vocational education is conducive to vocational education adapting to the rapidly updating market demand and changes, and training talents accurately. The relevant policies of the Vocational Education Law of the People's Republic of China have long stipulated that the financing channels of vocational education should be diversified, but at present the financial education funds and career income are still the main funding sources of vocational education in China. Therefore, it is necessary to further encourage individuals and enterprises to diversify their investment and further expand the channels of financing vocational education. Establishing private vocational school, for example, to run by the local vocational education development to create good competition environment, governments at all levels may according to the local people vocational education development, in the special financial vocational education funds according to certain proportion to arrange private vocational education funding, actively support the development of non-governmental vocational colleges in accords with a condition; Further promote school–enterprise cooperation, expand cooperation in running schools, order training, and realize diversified financing of vocational education through the diversification of funds in the training process. The government can formulate relevant laws and regulations to clarify the responsible subjects and ways of raising funds for vocational education. Strengthen international cooperation and seek financial support from international organizations; Preferential policies shall be formulated for land used for construction of vocational education, and measures shall be taken to support the development of vocational education, such as the return of land transfer fees and the mitigation of land-use fees. In addition, the government encourages healthy competition among vocational colleges, training institutions and industrial enterprises that provide vocational education and training in the form of purchasing vocational education services, so as to improve the efficiency of the use of funds and the quality of personnel training. Training institutions, vocational colleges and other efforts to improve the quality of teaching for public financial funds, not only to meet the people's needs for education, but also to increase the available funds of vocational colleges, to achieve a win–win situation.

4.4.5   Strengthening Supervision and Management of Funds for Vocational Education

The investment of educational funds is closely related to its supervision and management. A good financial investment system of vocational education cannot be established without the supervision and management of relevant government departments. When social groups and individuals are allowed and encouraged to participate in vocational education, it does not mean that the government completely passively allows it to develop freely. Governments at all levels and departments concerned must strictly implement laws and regulations related to vocational education funds and ensure that all laws are complied with; Formulate and implement the budget scientifically, realize the scientific management of vocational education funds, and improve the efficiency of the use of funds; Earnestly fulfill the management responsibility, and constantly improve the level of funds management. In addition, supervision is an important link. The government and relevant departments must disclose financial information in accordance with relevant regulations and accept social supervision to ensure that the use of funds meets safe, standard and effective standards. The central and local governments should establish corresponding institutions respectively to supervise and inspect the input and use of vocational funds. The local governments should regularly announce to the society the use of the budgetary funds of vocational education in all cities, counties and districts. The government can warn schools that violate the rules in terms of income and use of funds, and even introduce an exit mechanism to eliminate vocational schools that fail to fulfill their educational obligations. At the same time, we should give full play to the advantages of talents and intensive intelligence of the NPC and CPPCC. Before the enactment of major projects involving education every year and the appropriation of funds, the state should arrange members of the corresponding level and relevant experts to participate in the approval and evaluation of projects, to realize the social supervision of the input and use of education funds (Dong, 2016; Fang, 2007; Hu, 2020; Nian & Pan, 2019; Li, 2012; Qiu, 2011; Shen, 2018; Yuan & He, 2019; Zhang, 2010, 2011; Zhu, 2014).

References

Dong, F. (2016). Analysis of national financial investment in higher vocational education in China. *Vocational Education Research, 20*(5), 26–29.

Fang, L. (2007). Current situation and problems of the financial system of secondary vocational education. *Continuing Education Research, 20*(1), 67–70.

Hu, M. (2020). Research on financial policy of vocational education in China: Review. *Review and Prospect. Vocational Education Communication, 20*(6), 36–46.

Li, X. (2012). Analysis of investment in higher vocational education in China. *Education research, 33*(2), 49–52.

Nian, Y, & Pan, J. (2019). Comparison and enlightenment of vocational education financing mechanisms in The United States, Germany and Japan. *Vocational and Technical Education, 40*(12), 67–73.

Qiu, X. (2011). Study on the financial equity of secondary vocational education in China—Also on the free policy of secondary vocational education and its improvement. *Vocational Education Forum, 20*(6), 29–32.

Shen, Y. (2018). Analysis on the difference of vocational education funding allocation in recent ten years. *China Vocational and Technical Education, 20*(3), 66–75.

Yuan, L, & He, T. (2019). A review and evaluation of the reform of education finance system in China. *The Economics of Education Review, 4*(1), 11–37.

Zhang, W. (2010). Analysis and related thinking on the current situation of secondary vocational education funding in China. *Educational Research of Tsinghua University, 31*(2), 119–124.

Zhang, Y. (2011). Research on the financial policy of developing vocational higher education. *Institute of Fiscal Science, 10*(1), 112–119.

Zhu, A. (2014). Vocational education funding guarantee under the background of fiscal and tax system reform. *Vocational Education Forum, 20*(16), 4–8.

Chapter 5
The Student Financial Aid in China's Vocational Education

This chapter analyzes the student financial aid in China's vocational education. Vocational education is an important part of China's education, for China's economic and social development, personnel training to make an important contribution. Based on the 2012–2019 Report on the development of student financial aid in China, this study sorted out the policy texts of student financial aid for vocational education in the past 15 years and found that the degree of funding accuracy was low, education was insufficient and the source of funds needed to be enriched, and put forward some suggestions for these problems. In the domestic existing research results, scholars for vocational education student funding research content mainly focus on four aspects; First, the establishment and development of financial aid policy system for secondary vocational students; Second, the study of secondary vocational students in the implementation of financial aid policy problems and related countermeasures; Third, the effect evaluation of the implementation of vocational education funding policy; Fourth, we will study the financial aid policies for students from poor families in vocational colleges.

5.1 Literature Review

5.1.1 Research on the Formulation of Financial Aid Policies for Secondary Vocational Students

Fan et al. (2019) reviewed the formation and development process of China's student financial aid policies for vocational education in the past 70 years since the founding of the People's Republic of China, summarized the specific ways of student financial aid, and formed a summary of experience based on the achievements of China's student financial aid work. Xue and Xie (2018) analyzed the gradual updating and improvement of financial aid policies for secondary vocational students since China's reform and opening up. This paper summarizes two characteristics of the evolution of subsidy policy for secondary vocational schools in China and proposes to achieve the fair goal of subsidy policy for secondary vocational schools from the aspects of top-level design, precise policy, perfect value positioning, function optimization and coverage expansion. Gong and Qiu (2018) divided the development of subsidy system for secondary vocational schools in the past 40 years of reform and opening up into four stages and proposed that the subsidy system for secondary vocational schools had deficiencies in system, identification standard, students' comprehensive quality training and social participation. On this basis, it is suggested that China's secondary vocational subsidy policy system should be constructed from the following aspects: updating the concept, strengthening the function of the government and encouraging the social participation. The research on the evolution of the financial aid policy for students in vocational education provides a very systematic and perfect theoretical context for future research and can also reflect the continuous progress and improvement of the historical process of the financial aid for students in vocational education in China. It provides a detailed and solid literature basis for the formulation and research of the financial aid policy for students in vocational education in the future.

5.1.2   Research on the Implementation of Financial Aid Policy for Secondary Vocational Students

Scholars' research on the problems in the implementation of vocational education funding policy basically takes a province or a school as the research object. Many studies put forward countermeasures from four aspects: strengthening policy orientation, strengthening team building, formulating laws and regulations and paying attention to subsidizing education, so as to solve the problems in subsidizing management of secondary vocational schools. To promote the optimization of cohesive student financial aid in vocational and secondary vocational colleges, the measures of cohesive student financial aid, the promotion of vocational student financial aid policy, the strengthening of personnel allocation and the sharing of financial aid information are proposed (Dai, 2021; Song, 2018).

5.1.3   Research on the Effect Evaluation of Financial Aid Policy for Secondary Vocational Students

Since 2005, China formally put forward the "establishment of vocational education system for poor students" since the secondary vocational assistance policy has been implemented for more than a decade. Secondary vocational funding policy in the specific implementation of the effect is also the focus of scholars (Xing, 2021). Wei (2021) investigates zhunyi student financial assistance policy implementation in higher vocational colleges, students' recognition, satisfaction and fairness of the evaluation, and so on and so forth, analysis of the benefits of higher vocational colleges and universities student financial assistance policy implementation effect, existing problems and reasons, higher vocational colleges to improve the student aid policy system and improve implementation effect to provide the reference.

5.1.4 Research on Financial Aid Policies for Students from Poor Families in Vocational Colleges

With the expansion of the enrollment scale of higher vocational colleges, the number of poor students is gradually increasing. It has become an important measure to realize educational equity to do a good job in student financial aid in vocational colleges. Song (2018) analyzed the shortcomings and problems in the current student financial aid work in vocational colleges and made in-depth thinking and continuous exploration on new mechanisms, new approaches and new methods for accurate financial aid work for poor students. We should improve the financial aid system for students in higher vocational colleges, establish and improve the mechanism of precise identification and financial aid under the perspective of targeted poverty alleviation, combine poverty alleviation with aspiration and wisdom, promote the implementation of financial aid policies for students from poor families, do a good job in financial aid and ideological education for poor students and promote their growth and talents. Xing (2021) analyzed the current situation of student financial aid in higher vocational colleges, and put forward countermeasures from the aspects of improving the identification system of poor students, strengthening the construction of financial aid team, and giving full play to the function of financial aid and education. Wei (2021) pointed out that the current identification system for students from poor families in higher vocational colleges needs to solve the problems such as the unreasonable identification method and the lack of effective supervision mechanism. In this regard, we should reform the identification system of students from poor families in higher vocational colleges, including constructing the identification mechanism of students from poor families, optimizing the identification working procedures of students from poor families and improving the identification and supervision mechanism of students from poor families. Song (2018) analyzed the shortcomings and problems in the current student financial aid in higher vocational colleges and made in-depth thinking and continuous exploration on new mechanisms, new approaches and new methods for accurate financial aid for poor students. We should improve the financial aid system for students in higher vocational colleges, establish and improve the mechanism of precise identification and financial aid under the perspective of targeted poverty alleviation, combine poverty alleviation with aspiration and wisdom, promote the implementation of financial aid policies for students from poor families, do a good job in financial aid and ideological education for poor students, and promote their growth and talents (Dai, 2021; Hua et al., 2020; Xu, 2016; Zhang, 2021).

5.2   Data Analysis

5.2.1   Establishment and Development of Financial Aid Policy System for Secondary Vocational Students

Since the beginning of the twenty-first century, to promote educational equity and social equity, the state has promulgated a series of student financial aid policies, constantly expanding the channels of financial aid for secondary vocational students, expanding the scope of financial aid, and increasing the amount of financial aid. The financial aid policies at the national level are becoming more and more perfect. Table 3.1 on the next page lists some of the policies and measures launched by the state in the financial aid for secondary vocational students since the beginning of this century. As can be seen from Table 3.1, the development of financial aid policies for secondary vocational students in China has gone through a process of gradual establishment, deepening and poverty alleviation. With the increasing of China's comprehensive national strength, the secondary vocational student financial assistance policy system constantly improves, increasing funding means, funding standards continue to improve, and funding for expanding coverage, more and more poor families secondary vocational students can enjoy the benefits of national aid policy, in order to improve the attraction of the secondary vocational education created the good policy environment. From the historical process, the development of financial aid policy for secondary vocational students in China has the characteristic of gradual progress. The new policies are implemented after gradual exploration based on the original policies. Based on maintaining the consistency of content, the new policies are adjusted and modified according to past experience, implementation costs, social environment, economic conditions and new contradictions, so that the funding policy system can be gradually improved.

5.2.2   Current Situation and Characteristics of Financial Aid for Secondary Vocational Students

In recent years, the national financial aid to secondary vocational students has been increasing, and the proportion of subsidized students has increased year by year, as shown in Table 3.2. According to the Interim Measures on the Administration of State Grants for Secondary Vocational Education, issued in 2006, the standard of state grants for secondary vocational education students is 1,000 yuan per academic year. Published in 2007 "national secondary vocational school grants management interim measures", mark secondary national financial aid policy in the country, the full implementation of the funded object is "a secondary vocational school full-time formally admitted to the university of the first and second grade in school all the students in the rural household registration and county town of non-agricultural registered permanent residence and urban family economic difficulties students". The subsidy standard is 1500 yuan per student per year. 2009 national policy of secondary vocational education free tuition, object to public secondary school full-time formally admitted to the university student in grade one, two, three rural family economic difficulties students and agricultural majors (with the exception of arts performance-related majors), and also provides the implementation of regional and local and regional scale, free tuition subsidy funds, According to the standard of 2000 per student per year, the central government will share the amount with local governments in proportion. In 2010, the coverage of free tuition was further expanded to include secondary vocational school students from poor urban families. Since the beginning of the fall semester in 2012, free tuition funding continued to expand the coverage to all rural students (including county town), the urban agricultural professional and family economic difficulties students (with the exception of arts performance-related majors), and at the same time adjust national grant object for full-time formally admitted to the university in grade one, two and non-agriculture agricultural majors' family economic difficulties students. In other words, the scope of tuition-free financial aid has been further expanded, the scope of national grants has been gradually narrowed, and the financial aid structure has been continuously optimized to achieve fairness and justice. According to the Notice of the Ministry of Finance and Education on adjusting the policy on scholarships and grants for vocational schools, the national scholarship for secondary vocational education will be established from 2019 to reward outstanding full-time students in secondary vocational schools (including technical schools). 20,000 students will be awarded every year, the standard is 6000 yuan per student per year, highlighting the country's increasing attention to secondary vocational education. Secondary vocational national scholarship coverage is relatively narrow, the meaning of "award" is far more than the amount of "gold". For the award-winning students, this is an honor, but also a kind of affirmation and inspiration. The establishment of national scholarship for secondary vocational education is conducive to creating a social atmosphere that attaches importance to secondary vocational education. It can not only encourage the winners to sprint toward higher goals, but also motivate ordinary students to catch up with the standard and lead all secondary vocational students to follow the example. At this point, our country has formed tuition fees, grants, mainly to the national scholarship, local government funding, school funding and social assistance and other financial aid methods as auxiliary secondary vocational students financial aid system. The main sources of financial aid for secondary vocational students are government finance, social aid and on-the-job internship. In 2017 and 2018, 15.09992 million and 16.2970 million secondary vocational students were supported, with the amount of funding reaching 36.529 billion yuan and 39.996 billion yuan, up 9.98% and 9.49%, respectively. Of these, 99.852 million and 10.9833 million secondary vocational students were subsidized through tuition exemption, with 19.971 billion yuan and 21.966 billion yuan respectively. A total of 2.5476 million people and 2.82447 million people received state grants of 5.095 billion yuan and 5.618 billion yuan respectively. Local governments subsidized 870,500 people and 918,300 people with 681 million yuan and 836 million yuan, respectively. In addition, the school grants were 240 million yuan and 144 million yuan respectively, the social grants were 174 million yuan and 176 million yuan respectively, and the internship grants were 10.367 billion yuan and 11.256 billion yuan respectively. It can be seen from these data that the main source of financial aid for secondary vocational students is the financial input from central and local governments, while the investment from enterprises and public institutions and social organizations is less. In 2017 and 2018, national financial input accounted for 70.49% and 71.06% of the total financial aid for secondary vocational students, respectively. As national scholarships were established for secondary vocational education in 2019 and data related to in-post internship were excluded, government financial input accounted for 99.26% of the financial aid to secondary vocational students (Dai, 2021; Hua et al., 2020; Xu, 2016; Zhang, 2021).

5.3   Experience of Student Financial Aid Management in Developed Countries

5.3.1   The United States

The main characteristic of secondary vocational education in the United States is that it has a complete student financial aid system, no matter at which stage of students' study, there is a corresponding student financial aid system. Through this comprehensive financial aid, students can enjoy their study and enjoy the happiness brought by learning. What impresses us most is its scholarship system. The highest scholarship in the United States can not only exempt students from tuition and miscellaneous fees, but also exempt students from accommodation, insurance and book costs during their study, and also give a certain percentage of prize money to the winning students. Every year, the US government asks Congress for billions of dollars to start new vocational education programs. It also requires states to use the money to help build and develop secondary vocational schools, community colleges, and technical training schools.

5.3.2   Germany

The characteristics of student financial aid management in Germany are mainly reflected in its huge social strength to support students. Students are supported by individuals or organizations such as society and enterprises, so that students can understand the care of society for them and cultivate the idea of giving back to the society. German vocational education is also quite famous in the whole world. Vocational schools are public schools in Germany, and students can go to school free of charge. All the funds needed for running vocational schools are provided by governments at all levels and social enterprises. With the economic development, the German government's investment in vocational schools is also increasing year by year. According to German media reports, since the beginning of the twenty-first century, in order to solve the problem of youth unemployment without learning opportunities, the German government has decided to cooperate with enterprises, plus specific financial subsidies, to improve the enthusiasm of enterprises to participate in vocational education. In this way, in The German society, enterprises can use their social strength to promote vocational education, and the government will give certain subsidies to such enterprises to help them, and the young people trained to acquire certain knowledge, so as to repay the society (Dai, 2021; Hua et al., 2020; Xu, 2016; Zhang, 2021).

5.3.3 South Korea

South Korea's vocational student financial assistance system, its characteristic mainly reflects in South Korea for professional education fair policy is no matter who can go to professional school, and in a public vocational school, will not charge tuition and accommodation, only charge a cost, the student financial assistance system to the south Korean students undoubtedly brings strong study basis. Korean government departments will specifically designate some vocational schools, compulsory recruitment of a certain proportion of children from poor families, unemployed social personnel and the children of national meritorious personnel, among which the most important student financial aid mode is to award scholarships to outstanding students. Meanwhile, in the 1990s, to strengthen the popularity of vocational education, the South Korean government expanded the benefit rate of scholarship for vocational high school students, and added a certain proportion of financial aid, while providing preferential conditions for vocational school graduates in terms of admission and employment.

5.4 Challenges of Students' Financial Aid in Vocational Education

5.4.1 There are Problems in Financial Aid Policies for Secondary Vocational Students

Whether the policy of tuition exemption for secondary vocational schools or the national financial aid policy, its main financial aid function is mainly to help the poor, with universal and public welfare, and the incentive and guidance function of the policy is diluted. Even some schools for poor students to implement no difference in financial aid, not the organic combination of financial aid and education, did not let students understand in the enjoyment of rights at the same time to perform the corresponding obligations, leading to some students think that the enjoyment of financial aid is taken for granted, do not cherish, not frugal, not grateful. At present, the degree of precision of financial aid for secondary vocational students in China is relatively low. Most of them only stay at or even fail to reach the level of "precision of financial aid objects". There are few studies on the accuracy of regional, urban and rural, price and distribution quota differences. There are significant differences in economic and social development levels among the eastern, central and western regions. Without considering the resulting temporal and spatial differences in prices, the precision level of funding policies cannot be improved comprehensively and will inevitably lead to actual inequities.

5.4.2 The Target Group of the Subsidy Policy Needs to Be Further Expanded

At present, China has formed a financial aid system for secondary vocational students, including award, aid, exemption, loan, internship and social aid, and the relevant policies have been relatively sound. However, supporting policies and safeguards related to funding are still lacking. For example, how to effectively supervise and check the funding work, how to precisely allocate the funding funds, how to prevent the appropriation and misappropriation of the funding funds, whether the recipients use the funding funds reasonably, how to establish the withdrawal mechanism of the recipients, how to subsidize the poor students in private secondary vocational schools, and so on.

5.4.3 Sources of Student Financial Aid Need to Be Enriched

The financial aid for secondary vocational education students mainly comes from the national financial appropriation, and the proportion of social funds is very low, which objectively causes the dependence and habituality of secondary vocational schools on the government funding, and to some extent is also one of the reasons why the financial aid funds cannot be effectively used. With the development of national economy and the continuous progress of social civilization, social organizations, enterprises and institutions have been paying increasing attention to secondary vocational education and supporting students. Due to the lack of corresponding policy norms and guidance, this demand has not been effectively released.

5.4.4 The Lack of Effective Supervision and Evaluation System for Funding Management

Supervision and evaluation system is a very important link, and the current secondary vocational student financial aid management is exactly the lack of a perfect and effective supervision and evaluation system. All evaluation of student financial aid management is top-down, and achievement is achieved if policy tasks are accomplished. There is no specific supervision and evaluation on the content, effectiveness and fairness of student financial aid management, so students cannot easily feedback relevant information to the superior departments. The lack of effective supervision and evaluation system also restricts the development of funding management because the problems in management cannot be captured in time, and the possibility of solving the problems is lacking. It is often the case that a problem continues through several stages until the root of the problem cannot be traced.

5.4.5 The Identification of Poor Students Is Not Accurate Enough

China is a populous country. With the continuous expansion of college enrollment, there are more and more poor students in higher vocational colleges. How to identify the poor students in higher vocational colleges scientifically and reasonably, and then make full and effective use of financial support funds, is the primary problem to do a good job in student financial support. At present, the general process of identifying poor students in higher vocational colleges is as follows: the individual student submits the family economic situation questionnaire, the head teacher examines the materials, the class conducts democratic evaluation and the school (college) makes public announcement. These operations seem rigorous and meticulous, but there are some loopholes. Such as: Student personal list family economic conditions, if is by inputting tent card door, low, very poor worker children such as children, orphans, martyrs have related documents issued by the local civil affairs department, but the local economic development level is different, "poor students" from all over the world gathered in a region to determine the identity of a class, this standard is difficult to grasp; There are some general difficult family students, only by their own parents to fill in the income situation and other information, the teacher is unable to objectively go to the first review of the material; At the same time, with the expansion of enrollment in higher vocational colleges, the number of people applying for poor students in the class also gradually increased, even some class will be applied for more than half of the people, the class of the poor students democratic appraisal team appraisal result sometimes is not representative, or even a majority link will appear in some scattered, comment is invalid. Some students from rural areas who are really poor, such as student Jianlika, do not want their family economic situation to be known by their classmates due to inferiority complex and other reasons, but give up the opportunity to apply for financial aid. Moreover, the identification standard of poor students is vague, and some objective factors affect the evaluation of poverty grade of poor students (Dai, 2021; Hua et al., 2020; Xu, 2016; Zhang, 2021).

5.4.6   Insufficient Funding for Education

At present, higher vocational colleges are more inclined to subsidize education in the economic, the poor students' self-esteem and other psychological assistance is very little, but only in the material funding is far from enough. With the rapid development of economy and society, young people are under increasing physical and psychological pressure and have more and more troubles. The subsidized work of higher vocational colleges should not only be simple material, but also should take care of poor students' psychology, emotion, spirit and other aspects continuously. Some poor students have low self-esteem, sensitivity and pessimism, lack integrity consciousness and gratitude feelings, have no confidence in personal life development and do not have a clear plan for employment, etc., which means that the deepest educational function of funding work does not really play a role. For poor students, their emotional and social needs are more intense. They need to be cared for and respected. They need to realize themselves through rich social contacts and life experience, which cannot be realized only with simple financial aid. In 2018, General Secretary Xi Jinping stressed at the National Education Conference that what we train are socialist builders and successors, and the foundation of educating people lies in virtue. New era is facing the new situation and new development, the progress of the society and the country's development cannot leave the talents, higher vocational colleges and universities as the cradle of talent training, practical skills should keep pace with The Times, make full use of the fund management platform, real play to fund education function, for the society and national physique and a new era of comprehensive development of young talent (Dai, 2021; Hua et al., 2020; Xu, 2016; Zhang, 2021).

5.4.7 The Subvention Team Is Not Professional

At present, various higher vocational colleges throughout the country have set up student financial aid management centers in strict accordance with relevant requirements in practical work. However, in the actual work, there is a shortage of student financial aid staff, professionalism is not strong. At present, the financial support team of all kinds of colleges and universities is basically composed of a combination of full-time and part-time personnel from the assistant management department of student and salary, party secretaries, counselors and head teachers of secondary colleges in charge of student work. But in the team, having a plenty of professional part-time teachers, and a plenty of young student-specific work of instructors, their lack of work experience in student financial assistance, also does not have a good grasp and school funding work-related national policies and requirements, in the work that missing links, leakage misspelled comments, issues of public dissent; Due to the lack of experience in front-line student work management, the special staff of the student engineering department sometimes arranges the work mechanically, which leads to great pressure, low efficiency and many problems in the work of the secondary colleges. In addition, the policy and timeliness of the financial support work in higher vocational colleges are strong. Basically, the work requirements of each academic year will change, and the situation of students each year is also different, which puts forward higher requirements for the working ability and comprehensive quality of the financial support work team. Therefore, it is necessary to build a professional and research-oriented team who are proficient in the business and familiar with the profession part-time (Dai, 2021; Hua et al., 2020; Xu, 2016; Zhang, 2021).

5.5 Suggestions on the Development of Financial Aid for Secondary Vocational Students

5.5.1 Further Expanding the Target Group of the Fund

Secondary part funding policy is only for poor students in our country, and on the basis of national finance income rising, it can be appropriate to refer to other forms of compulsory education in our country, to the secondary vocational education to carry out the whole free education system, in the implementation stage, can according to the actual situation by the national finance, the local provincial and municipal financial situation as well as the national talent demand structure. We will introduce a model of free secondary vocational education and half-fee fees in some majors, and gradually introduce free secondary vocational education in light of the effect of implementation.

5.5.2 Give Full Play to the Incentive Effect of Funding Policies

At present, the universal financial aid policy in secondary vocational schools is not effective enough in stimulating students' enthusiasm for learning. We can learn from the experience of higher education students' financial aid, introduce the funding resource competition mechanism and the funding withdrawal mechanism, combine the aid to the poor, award and contribution, and strengthen the incentive effect of the financial aid policy. In addition to considering the student family economic conditions, but also should be personal assessment test scores, technical skills, comprehensive ethical factors including, establishing a comprehensive evaluation index system, funding for poor, poor, poor performance of student's appropriate deductions funding, funding competition mechanism become impetus to motivate the poor student's all-round development. The national scholarship policy for secondary vocational schools, which was implemented in 2019, is a useful attempt.

5.5.3 Improve the Precision of Funding Policies

It is necessary to deepen, refine and optimize the content of funding policies, balance the implementation capacity of various regions, provinces, and cities, and between urban and rural areas, and ensure the effectiveness and precision of funding policies. Secondly, we should improve the information management platform of student financial aid, make full use of big data technology, analyze the difference of economic difficulties between regions and among poor students in the same school, and realize the precision of financial aid allocation. Starting from 2019, the state grants for secondary vocational education began to be distributed by file in a comprehensive way. From the standard of 2000 yuan per student per year, they were distributed by file in the range of 1000–3000 yuan according to local conditions. Through a series of measures, deepen and refine the financial aid policy for secondary vocational students in China, promote the accurate development of financial aid for secondary vocational students, reduce the behavior of banding, misappropriating and misusing, and avoid the speculative behavior in the implementation of the policy (Dai, 2021; Hua et al., 2020; Xu, 2016; Zhang, 2021).

5.5.4 Actively Introduce Social Funding Resources

From the perspective of the long-term development of secondary vocational education, the state should introduce incentive policies as soon as possible to attract social capital into the secondary vocational funding system. This will not only reduce the financial pressure on the government, but also revitalize social funds, highlight the social responsibility of social groups and enthusiastic people, and form a good demonstration effect. Specific reference can be made to the policy guidance and legal constraints of the education funding system in western countries, to encourage enterprises, groups and social persons to donate to education through the establishment of funds, named scholarships, free donations, matching pledges and other ways, and gradually create a harmonious and strong social atmosphere of donation to education (Dai, 2021; Hua et al., 2020; Xu, 2016; Zhang, 2021).

5.5.5 *Improve the Poverty-Stricken Students Identification System*

The precise analysis and control should be carried out to ensure the authenticity of the family situation, economic situation and learning situation of the subsidized students, and strive to achieve relative justice and fairness. The honesty education should be strengthened, credit files should be established and dishonesty behaviors should be restricted and punished. For individual students' dishonest behaviors, schools should punish them according to the seriousness of the circumstances and the campus rules and student management regulations. Funding management in higher vocational colleges to create the database and continuously updated, has a poor student enrollment for dynamic assessment and management, to perfect information, academic performance, during the period of school served situation, participate in academic activities and work-study experience, part-time jobs data such as income and monthly cost of living, every school year a targeted grant. For lower-grade poor students, emphasis should be placed on economic assistance, because they have not fully adapted to college life and cannot quickly find suitable work-study positions or part-time jobs. For senior poor students, attention should be paid to ideological guidance and emotional motivation. For them, a satisfactory internship position, a mature career planning, and a confidence to achieve economic independence may be more attractive than thousands of yuan of financial aid every year. For the poor students whose living consumption increases month by month, we should give early warning and understand the situation in time. If the living consumption is in advance and the information is concealed, we should stop supporting them and guide them in time to help them establish the correct consumption concept and learn to plan their own life. For poor students with excellent grades, we should encourage them to actively participate in the application of scholarships at all levels, give them a platform to shine, cultivate their qualities of gratitude, solidarity with classmates and willingness to contribute and voluntarily give the quota to those who need it more. Developmental financial aid refers to a financial aid system that takes the fairness of education as the basis, the effectiveness of financial aid as the goal, and the development of students as the goal, through free financial aid such as financial support, psychological counseling, and the basic ways of paid assistance to students such as getting paid for work and improving their ability through practice. First, we should pay attention to the psychological dynamic changes of poor students, strengthen humanistic care and mental health education, provide psychological counseling channels for them, and help them establish a healthy psychological state. Homeroom teachers, counselors, mental health center teachers should regularly interview the poor students, through a variety of forms of counseling services, targeted psychological counseling for them, effectively solve their troubles in life.

5.5.6 Strengthen the Construction of the Financial Support Team

First, higher vocational colleges can introduce teachers with professional backgrounds to work on school funding management. The poor students are a special group in higher vocational colleges, they not only need financial support, but also need spiritual and life guidance, as a result, fund management workers can't focus on the complicated transactional work, want to often, bow their heads and thinking, into the daily work experience into theory and method of concise results, enhance the level of work and scientific research ability. Higher vocational colleges should pay attention to cultivate high level of business and professional background of finance management workers, has introduced politics, pedagogy, psychology, management science, statistics and other professional background of teachers engaged in school funding management related work, building a research fund management team, to the poor student's education and management of all, to ensure that funding education is ongoing and effective everywhere. Secondly, to further enhance the professionalism of student financial aid managers, vocational colleges should organize regular or irregular training for student financial aid managers. In addition, we can send our student financial aid administrators to domestic higher vocational colleges with better student financial aid management to visit and study, learn from others' beneficial experience, and make up for their own deficiencies in student financial aid management (Dai, 2021; Hua et al., 2020; Xu, 2016; Zhang, 2021).

References

Dai, Y. (2021). The implementation status and countermeasures of student financial aid policy in the context of the connection between middle and higher vocational colleges. *Modern Vocational Education, 20*(3), 182–183.

Fan, X., Tang, B., & Guo, Q. (2019). *Journal of Central China Normal University (Humanities and Social Sciences Edition), 201*(5), 1–15.

Gong, Y., & Qiu, X. (2018). Review and prospect of financial aid system for secondary vocational students in China in 40 years of reform and opening up. *Education Guide, 20*(5), 92–96.

Hua, J., Liu, W., Guo, L., Han, Y. (2020). Analysis on the current situation and problems of student financial aid in secondary vocational schools. *Vocational Education (Mid-day), 19*(12), 7–10.

Song, Y. (2018). Reflections on student financial support in higher vocational colleges in the new era. *The Wind Science and Technology, 20*(3), 38–39.

Wei, X. (2021). Research on the identification system of students from Families with economic difficulties in higher vocational colleges. *Education and Vocational Education, 20*(10), 105–108.

Xing, Y. N. (2021). Current situation and countermeasures of student financial support in higher vocational colleges. *Textile and Garment Education, 36*(2), 187–190.

Xu, C. (2016). Research on the construction of developmental funding system for college students in China. *Party Building and Ideological Education in Schools, 20*(5), 57–59.

Xue, R., & Xie, C. (2018). The evolution and prospect of financial aid policy for secondary vocational students in China in the past 40 years of reform and opening. *Education and Vocational Education, 20*(17), 36–41.

Zhang, L. (2021). Research on identification of disadvantaged students in colleges and universities under the new student financial aid policy. *Educational Observation, 10*(1), 127–129.

Chapter 6
Chinese Vocational Education Examination and Enrollment System

This chapter examines Chinese vocational education exam and enrollment system from different perspectives. As an important part of China's education system, vocational education plays an important role in cultivating diverse technical talents and promoting employment. As one of the most important links in the development of vocational education, the examination and enrollment system has been paid more and more attention by the state. It is of great theoretical value and practical significance to study the system of vocational education examination and enrollment. By consulting the relevant literature and comparing the development model of vocational education with that of other developed countries in the world, this chapter aims to provide reasonable countermeasures and suggestions for the enrollment and examination system of vocational education in China.

6.1 Literature Review

6.1.1 Research on Policy Changes of Vocational Education Examination and Enrollment System Reform

On May 5, 2010, the Executive meeting of The State Council deliberated and adopted the Outline of the National Medium- and Long-term Education Reform and Development Plan (2010–2020), which proposed to "gradually form the examination and enrollment system of classified examination, comprehensive evaluation and multiple admission; Secondary vocational schools enroll students or register for admission independently, and the entrance examination for higher vocational education is organized by the provinces, autonomous regions and municipalities directly under the

Central Government". On April 15, 2013, the Ministry of Education issued the Guidance of the Ministry of Education on Actively Promoting the Reform of the Examination and Enrollment System of Higher Vocational Education, proposing that "Gradually separate from the undergraduate examination of ordinary colleges and universities, focus on exploring the examination and evaluation method of 'knowledge + skills', and provide diversified enrollment forms for students to receive higher vocational education. We will gradually form a higher vocational education examination and enrollment system with Chinese characteristics, featuring students' independent selection, diversified enrollment and effective social supervision". At the same time, suggestions on six ways of higher vocational education entrance examination are given. On September 4, 2014, The State Council issued the Implementation Opinions on Deepening the Reform of the Examination and Enrollment System, which clearly pointed out that "the examination and enrollment of higher vocational colleges are relatively separate from ordinary colleges and universities, and the evaluation method of 'cultural literacy + vocational skills' is implemented". On February 13, 2019, The State Council issued the National Implementation Plan for Vocational Education Reform, which proposed to "improve the development level of secondary vocational education; We will establish a vocational education college entrance examination system, improve the examination and enrollment method of 'cultural literacy + vocational skills', and provide students with a variety of entrance and learning methods for higher vocational education". The above series of policies highlight the importance of vocational education in the education system and provide guidance for the further deepening of the reform of vocational education. Vocational education should be placed on an equal footing with ordinary higher education.

6.1.2 Domestic Research on Vocational Education Examination and Enrollment System

By reading the literature, it is found that the domestic literatures about vocational education examination system are mainly concentrated in the higher vocational education, there is less research on secondary vocational education, through the induction summary, research on vocational exam system mostly concentrated in the following aspects: one is for the macroscopic research of higher vocational education examination recruitment system, including system reform, admissions standards; The second is from the perspective of independent enrollment, including five forms; Third, from the perspective of diversity, to seek a diversified recruitment form. Firstly, starting from the examination and enrollment system of vocational education itself, Wang and Ding (2012) revealed the problems in the system design, examination content and attractiveness of higher vocational education from the current situation of the system, and gave specific suggestions for reform. They believed that vocational orientation testing tools should be developed; Reduce the unified examination subjects, to the transition of multiple admission; Expand the scope and scale of self-recruitment; Expand the single enrollment scale, improve the linkage mechanism between middle and higher vocational colleges; Reasonably reduce tuition fees and establish a "green channel" for middle - and low-income classes to enter the school. Yuan and Chai (2016) pointed out that the current examination and enrollment system of higher vocational education exposed problems such as unreasonable enrollment structure, emphasis on cultural orientation and decrease of students. It is necessary to change ideas and take measures such as relaxing admission conditions, optimizing enrollment structure and adjusting the ratio of general employment to general employment. Zhao (2006) discussed the current situation of higher vocational college enrollment examination and proposed the idea of "classifying and stratifying enrollment, reforming examination subjects and examination content". Li (2017) pointed out that the vocational college examination and enrollment system is faced with problems such as insufficient selectivity, unclear reform impetus of examination and enrollment, unclear identity of subjects, uncertain examination and enrollment supervision and uncertainty of examination content. The reform should be carried out in the aspects of system supply quality, examination, and enrollment form, etc. Yang (2006) pointed out that the recruitment of students test problem not only exists in the examination system itself, but there are also on the running mechanism, the current reform of the goal should be to increase the effectiveness and pertinence of recruit students, improve the basic and comprehensive exam content, realize the examination way diversification, and put forward "exam + single test" mode in order to increase the number. Sha (2002) through the reform of the system of research in recent years, the recruitment of student's test, found our students' lack of unity, lack of pertinence, entrance standard single exam sexual problems such as lack of cohesion, put forward the common higher education and higher vocational education "the two towers, bimodal and texts", establish "cross up counterpart, down" the reform of the system of new ideas. Li (2006) discussed the reform of the examination system in higher vocational colleges from four aspects: the concept of examination, the content of examination, the method of examination and the reward mechanism. He proposed to update the examination concept and establish an examination system based on quality education and professional technology, supplemented by flexible and diversified examination forms. Lai starting from the design and implementation of the self-admission examination system, believed that classified examination and parallel admission should be further improved. Broaden the range of higher vocational students; Give full play to the role of vocational education groups to form a unified system of enrollment standards; Establish a unified test (test) testing platform, independently determine the test combination and requirements (Fan, 2010; Lai, 2009; Li, 2006; Liang, 2011; Sha, 2002; Wang, 2011; Wang & Ding, 2012; Xue & Li, 2020; Yang, 2006; Yuan & Chai, 2016; Zhao, 2006).

Wang (2011) believes that the public should timely reflect on the current enrollment system, pointing out that the independent enrollment of higher vocational colleges is the decentralization of state power, and schools should shoulder greater responsibilities. Fan (2010) expounded the adverse effects of higher vocational college enrollment relying on the unified college entrance examination system, analyzed the importance of independent enrollment from two aspects of theoretical basis and realistic demands, and put forward the preliminary conception of independent enrollment reform. Liang (2011) pointed out that in the independent enrollment selection mechanism, "the interview and assessment are single, the written test content focuses on basic cultural knowledge and ignores the professional quality assessment".

Finally, the study of vocational education examination system from the perspective of diversification. Through the summary of relevant literature on vocational education examination and enrollment system, it can be found that the current research on this issue lacks integrity and coordination. Most scholars focus their research content on a specific link or one aspect, and the research methods are more limited to their own experience and lack sufficient theoretical support. The overall research level of the vocational education examination system is insufficient. How to promote the design and reform of the vocational education examination system still needs our further thinking.

6.2 International Comparison of Vocational Education Examination

6.2.1 Japanese Vocational Education Examination System

Japan's vocational education system is mainly composed of three parts, namely school education, enterprise education and social education under the school, enterprise education and social education system. School education is the main body of Japanese vocational education, including secondary vocational education and higher vocational education two stages. At present, Japan has shifted the focus of vocational education from secondary vocational education to higher vocational education and regards higher vocational education as an important part of higher education. Whether it is private or public, the examination and enrollment methods of higher vocational colleges in Japan mainly involve three types: general entrance examination, recommended entrance examination and AO examination. The general entrance examination is a national unified examination, the results of which can be used as the basis for admission to regular colleges and higher vocational colleges. The remaining two are based on the vocational ability of the students, the targeted assessment of the admitted students.

The general entrance examination is mainly divided into two stages: the university entrance examination and the secondary examination in school. The College Entrance Examination is a national unified entrance examination held by the College Entrance Center. It mainly examines students' mastery of basic knowledge and skills in high school. Exam content proposition by the college entrance examination center, unified national life, including geological history, language, science, foreign languages, mathematics, citizens six disciplines, a total of 30 subjects (see Table 3.1), center for exams since 1990, has a history of more than 30 years, until 2021, center of the examination will be replaced by the common university entrance exam. The subject of the common examination remains the same, but some adjustments have been made in the content and time of the examination of specific subjects, and more emphasis has been placed on the examination of students' thinking ability. The secondary examination in school is an examination form organized by each school according to its own characteristics. Students can take the secondary examination in the volunteer school according to the actual situation after taking the central examination. Generally, different schools have different examination subjects and selection methods, including interviews, small papers, written tests and other forms. As a supplement to the general entrance examination, the recommended entrance examination is mainly based on written materials such as letters of recommendation which can reflect the students' academic achievements. It was initially used by private universities, then gradually expanded to short-term universities, and is now used by higher vocational colleges. It is the second largest admission method after the general entrance examination. (1) appoint school to recommend, namely higher vocational school designates the graduate of partial school to attend. (2) Open recruitment. This is a recommendation method for students who have not been recommended by a designated school or no designated school. Students who have graduated from high school, students who have graduated from junior high school in a five-year system of higher education or those who have completed courses in an educational institution with the same level of education as a junior high school are eligible to participate in this type of recommendation. (3) Self-recommendation. Different from the previous two methods of recommendation written by the school and the principal, self-recommendation requires students to write their own recommendation and be assessed through written review and interview (Fan, 2010; Lai, 2009; Li, 2006; Liang, 2011; Sha, 2002; Wang, 2011; Wang & Ding, 2012; Xue & Li, 2020; Yang, 2006; Yuan & Chai, 2016; Zhao, 2006).

The AO stands for The Admissions Office in Japan, which refers to the "selection method based on a comprehensive assessment of candidates' ability, suitability, desire and sense of purpose". This approach focuses on two-way selection between students and universities based on students' knowledge of the schools they are applying to. It fully respects students' learning characteristics and willingness, and comprehensively evaluates students from various aspects. Therefore, it is also called "comprehensive selection entrance exam". Japanese higher vocational colleges evaluate students through the national General Entrance Examination, AO Entrance Examination and recommended Entrance Examination, and enroll students through three forms of regular admission, selection admission and special admission. The conventional admission method is frequently used in the process of college admission. Different schools demarcate different admission scores according to the characteristics of schools and majors. However, as the most unified test in Japan, most students will take the university Entrance Center test and get the corresponding score index. In the process of admission, different majors in different universities will determine different admission standards according to the characteristics of their majors. For example, different course combinations will be set for different majors. In addition to the fixed course requirements, the rest can be freely matched to meet the requirements and requirements of students to the greatest extent. The general entrance examination can be divided into two stages. After the entrance examination at the university entrance center, students can take the second in-school examination according to their own wishes. The second examination can not only choose a more flexible testing method, but also play a role of diversion to match students into more suitable majors. The unity and universality of the central examination make the conventional admission method become the most used admission method in colleges and vocational schools, greatly simplifying the admission process. The biggest characteristic of the selection admission method is batch admission and multi-major combination admission. Different schools will develop a variety of admission standards according to the actual situation, including comprehensive consideration of all the data of students, and develop specific admission standards for different majors. Students choose the most suitable major according to their own will, and obtain the admission qualification through the professional assessment, so as to achieve the matching of the major and candidates. This way of admission highlights the two-way choice between the school and the student, reducing the possibility of students and majors being unmatched, is a further complement to the regular admission method.

Special admission methods are mainly aimed at students with specific abilities. They mainly include range admission and non-quantitative conditional admission. The scope of admission mainly refers to the selection of students with ability in a certain aspect, which can be a certain subject, or a certain professional ability. The school sets high assessment requirements for different aspects. Students who pass the assessment can be admitted directly without any other written test results. Non-quantified conditional admission mainly refers to a way for schools to admit students after comprehensive consideration of materials that can prove students' ability and quality, such as recommendation letters from authoritative people and students' learning experience. To sum up, the special admission method can ensure that students with special talents or recommended students can enter the school for further development and avoid the loss of the right to education for students unable to enter the school due to partial subjects or other reasons. In a word, the three enrollment methods of Japanese vocational colleges and universities, on the basis of the general parallel enrollment, make use of diversified admission methods according to the particularity of students, and satisfy the two-way choice between students and schools.

6.2.2 The German

The German vocational school system is huge and complex. From bottom to top, it is mainly divided into three main channels of vocational education, which are divided and connected with each other, and finally correspond to three types of technical (vocational) colleges, higher vocational colleges (applied technical universities) and universities/technical universities. In the learning process starting from primary school, learners can change to different types of schools at any time according to their own interests and development, to ensure the personalized development of each person. The German education system is divided into five stages. In these five stages, students go through three triage and finally decide on their own learning direction. First shunt occurred after completing four years of primary school education stage, students do not need to get through the unified exam, but according to their own ability, the overall performance of the process of learning, the teacher's advice, etc., in the main school, Realschule choices, complete high school and comprehensive school, middle school to practice training is given priority to, complete secondary school with cultural teaching is given priority, practical secondary school and comprehensive secondary school are the combination of the two, this diversion process can generally last 1–2 years, students can choose several times, and then enter the secondary education stage. The second diversion occurs when students are 16 to 19 years old. Again, students do not need to pass the unified examination. Students choose between general education and vocational education according to their junior high school education. Students who take the vocational education route are enrolled in dual vocational schools and full-time vocational schools, as well as some vocational schools with "overpass function". The third diversion occurs at the end of high school education and the stage of higher education. There are three types of colleges and universities for students to choose namely comprehensive universities, colleges and vocational colleges. Higher vocational education in Germany is mainly implemented by higher vocational colleges and vocational colleges. Higher vocational colleges are a higher technical education mode based on traditional universities by absorbing some characteristics of vocational education, while vocational colleges are the main body of "dual system" vocational education mode. It is a new form of higher technical education jointly organized by the enterprises and the government. The diplomas issued by the graduates of the two kinds of universities are equivalent. Admission to a junior college is open to students who have graduated from a junior high school or other high school (liberal arts high school) and have some professional experience that qualifies them for junior college admission. The entrance qualification of junior high school graduates is mainly obtained through the graduation examination, which is divided into two parts: the written examination includes German, mathematics, foreign language and any other subject, and the oral examination includes the written subject and a subject related to the professional course. Vocational colleges adopt the "dual system" mode of vocational education, the "dual" of the "dual system" is mainly reflected in the cooperation between training enterprises and schools in vocational education and related training tasks. There are two main ways for vocational colleges to recruit: first, graduates with higher school diplomas are enrolled through signing training contracts with enterprises; The second is for the social personnel with the same social education through training, after passing the relevant entrance test and signing the training contract.

6.2.3 The United States

The typical characteristic of American vocational education is decentralized management, and community colleges occupy the main position. Community college is the original system of education, was originally called "junior college", mainly provides supplementary education, technical degrees and certificates, high school degree, at the same time because its signed four-year college or university with a number of "2 + 2 credit transfer agreement", students can also through the community college, electronic transfer credits to subsequent four-year colleges, and receive a bachelor's degree. Unlike community colleges, American technical colleges offer more training in specific vocational skills. Students who graduate from technical colleges can earn certificates or degrees. In the United States, standardized test scores are required for admission to higher education, and these test scores are also applicable to the special assessment standards and requirements of vocational schools. Currently, vocational schools recognize six standardized tests related to Test admissions, including the main SAT and ACT, as well as the CLEP and The Preliminary Scholastic Assessment Test (PSAT), AP exam and International Baccalaureate Diploma Programme (IB). The SAT, also known as the College Entrance Examination, is a high school scholastic aptitude test administered by the College Board. It is an important indicator of admission to US colleges and universities. The SAT i, which focuses on the reasoning test, is a test of learning ability. It is designed to test a student's ability to adapt to college education. It is also a required score for applying to American universities. The test, which includes four sections: reading, grammar, math and writing, is currently based on a revised version introduced in 2016, with a total score of 1,600, with a full score of 800 for math, 400 for both reading and grammar, and a separate score of 24 for the writing section. The test will take three hours in reading, grammar and math, and 50 min in writing as an optional section. The SAT ii, also sponsored by the College Board, is a subject test with 20 subjects in five units in English, history, math, science and languages. The SAT ii is not required for college applications. Colleges that require SAT ii scores will require two or three scores.

The PSAT, also known as the preparatory SAT, is a test that students take before taking the SAT. The PSAT is based on the content of the SAT i before the 2005 redesign. The PSAT can be used to predict future SAT scores. The PSAT scores can also be compared with future SAT scores as a standard of matching. Third, students with excellent grades (the top 10% in each state) can apply for American scholarships, accounting for about 0.5% of all students taking the test. The ACT test is administered by ACT INC, a private, nonprofit company in the United States. Like the SAT, it is accepted by almost every college in the United States. The ACT consists of five sections in English, Math, Reading, Science and Writing (optional), with a total score of 36. It is a comprehensive test of students' ability to take basic courses. Because the SAT and ACT scores are interchangeable, students can submit test scores in their favor. AP tests, or Advanced Placement courses, are administered by the College Board, and good AP scores can also be used to deduct credits for courses taken in college. The test content mainly involves 37 courses of 22 majors, divided into multiple choice questions and free answers. The final scoring standard is 1–5 points, with 5 being the highest score. Generally, a score of more than 3 points can be admitted to most schools. The IB exams are administered by the International Baccalaureate Organization (IBO) and cover a range of subjects from primary, secondary to high school, as well as vocational education. Students who pass the exam will receive an International Baccalaureate, an alternative to a first-year university course. The IBDP program is a two-year program designed specifically for college students and is accepted by hundreds of universities in the United States. The CLEP is a college-level examination system sponsored by the College Board and administered by the Educational Testing Service.

Community colleges in the United States have not set up a special national examination and admission agency, and students do not need to take a test to enter community colleges. This open admission policy provides great convenience for students. In addition, community college enrollment and enrollment time is not subject to the national and state government jurisdiction, the community college is open to students at the beginning of each semester, as long as the students meet the requirements can apply. Community college enrollment mainly includes the community or the state of the general high school graduates, graduates of secondary vocational and technical colleges and some working experience of on-the-job personnel. Recruitment standards are mainly based on the needs and interests of students. Strictly speaking, community colleges in the United States have absolute autonomy in the recruitment process, which is further favored by students. But an open enrollment mechanism does not mean absolute "freedom". Out of consideration "selective" American community colleges in the admissions process put forward clear requirements, namely "all bachelor's degree majoring in part and associate degree majored in recruits only particular people", this kind of student requires a certain academic ability and prerequisites and academic performance to meet certain standards. Community colleges typically require professional. Applicants are required to submit evidence within a specified period of time. Students can indicate this by listing their highest achievements over the course of their academic career and submitting relevant standardized test scores.

6.2.4 British

Britain is a typical country with "certificate system". Its vocational education system focuses on national vocational qualifications and builds a strict vocational education system oriented by vocational qualifications. It is connected with general education horizontally and forms a bottom-up system vertically, which provides an important guarantee for students' further study and employment. The British education system is mainly divided into three stages: compulsory education, further education and higher education. Compulsory education includes primary education and secondary education, while vocational education is mainly concentrated in the secondary education and further education stages of compulsory education. The GCSE certificate is the most common and important level 2 certificate in the United Kingdom. GCSEs are taken by all pupils who have completed compulsory education (at the age of 16) and are divided into seven grades: A–F, with an "A+" for exceptional academic performance, and a grade of C and above equivalent to a second level qualification, while the rest obtain a first level qualification. GCSE is not a comprehensive education certificate, but a subject certificate. The Department of Education requires all students to take at least five GCSEs. The number and grade of GCSEs are the basis for applying to higher education institutions. The BTEC is a vocational education certificate issued by the Technical Education Council of the Council for Industry and Commerce in the United Kingdom. It covers a wide range of secondary and higher education. The BTEC is administered by Edexis Qualifications and Vocational Qualifications, which covers 17 vocational and technical areas, including art and design, business and architecture, at levels from Level 1 to Level 8 of the UK qualifications framework. GNVQ certificates are different levels of certificates and courses designed by the UK Department for Education for students aged 14–16 (later stages of compulsory education) and those aged 17–19 entering colleges of further education. GNVQ vocational qualifications are divided into courses and exams at a number of levels, including elementary, intermediate and advanced, and each level requires two years of study. The junior GNVQ program requires students to complete 9 units, including 3 required vocational units, 3 elective vocational units and 3 Level 1 Core competency units; Intermediate GNVQ requires students to complete 10 units of competency, including 4 required vocational units, 3 elective vocational units and 3 Core Level 2 competency units; Advanced GNVQ requires completion of 15 units of competence, including 8 required vocational units, 4 elective vocational units and 3 Core Level 3 units. In the United Knigdom, as in most countries, the ultimate power of admission lies with the institution itself. British vocational holds on very open recruitment system, it faces the recruit students object is very extensive, as long as at least 18 years of age, and holds GNVQ junior or intermediate certificate, certificate of BTEC first, BTEC national vocational certificate, three or more GCSE certificates or other can prove that the applicant has completed general secondary education or secondary vocational and technical education certificate, you can enter the Institute of Further Education for higher vocational and technical education.

In addition to colleges and universities, there is an organization called the University and College Admissions Service (UCAS) which provides help with admissions. The organization has three basic functions: one is to provide application and registration service. Besides helping students submit their application for admission, it also provides student counseling service. The second is to provide a variety of certificates for score conversion. Third, to assist schools in the admission work, for the students who did not accept timely adjustment (Fan, 2010; Lai, 2009; Li, 2006; Liang, 2011; Sha, 2002; Wang, 2011; Wang & Ding, 2012; Xue & Li, 2020; Yang, 2006; Yuan & Chai, 2016; Zhao, 2006).

6.2.5 *China*

In China, the unified enrollment of secondary vocational schools mostly means that the state takes out a certain range of quotas for secondary vocational schools, and vocational schools recruit students for junior middle schools. The object of unified recruit is to participate in unified junior high school graduation entrance examination of students, namely the so-called examinee, which did not reach the high school admission score line will enter the secondary vocational school to study. The unified recruitment of secondary vocational schools is very unified from the examination form to the admission method, and the examination content is mainly based on the complete theoretical knowledge, ignoring the investigation of the skill test. In addition to the high school entrance examination, China's secondary vocational enrollment also has directional enrollment, registration and enrollment and other ways, but generally speaking, there is not a separate examination and enrollment system, vocational education enrollment examination and high school enrollment examination mixed form is not conducive to the diversion of students and is not conducive to the healthy development of vocational education.

China has gradually paid more and more attention to the classified entrance examination system of higher vocational education. Since 2014, it has been repeatedly proposed to "gradually implement the classified entrance examination of higher vocational education" and "establish the enrollment system in line with the characteristics of vocational education". However, the development of higher vocational examination and enrollment system is still not mature enough. At present, the form of examination and enrollment in higher vocational colleges in China is still based on the college entrance examination mode, and a variety of auxiliary entrance methods coexist, but overall, it does not break away from the form of unified examination. Since the implementation of the college entrance examination, it has gone through many reforms, and the system has become more and more perfect, but in essence, it still cannot get rid of the labels of "only score theory" and "exam-oriented education". College entrance examination, as an examination and enrollment system for universities to select excellent talents, ignores vocational education in content and form, which is undoubtedly not conducive to the healthy development of vocational education. At present, the current college entrance examination in China takes the form of unified proposition in most regions, and independent proposition in some regions. The examination schemes mainly include "3+X" scheme, "3+3" scheme and "3+1+2" scheme. "3" is the traditional Chinese, mathematics, English three subjects, for the compulsory test items. "3+X" is the most widely used program at present. In addition to the traditional three subjects, "X" means that students can independently choose one of the two comprehensive subjects of liberal arts (politics, history and geography) and science (physics, chemistry, and biology) as the examination subject, with a total score of 750 points (150 points for each of the three subjects and 300 points for the comprehensive). "3+3" scheme is applied in Shanghai, Zhejiang, Beijing, Shandong, Tianjin and Hainan provinces; students from physics, history, politics, geography, biology and chemistry choose three of six subjects chosen to test for learning (Zhejiang for seven families), including technology, including three big subjects according to the original points, choose three test subjects rating assignment statement. In the "3+1+2" scheme, the "1" refers to physics or history, and the "2" refers to the two subjects in politics, geography, biology and chemistry. The total score is also calculated using the original and assigned points system. No matter what the program is, it cannot be separated from the nature of the examination based on the theoretical knowledge of cultural courses. The content of the examination is based on the investigation of theoretical knowledge, which also determines that the standard for higher vocational colleges to admit students is the students' college entrance examination results. At present, the admission score line of each province is determined in accordance with the overall enrollment plan of the current year and the distribution of candidates' scores. In terms of applying for universities and admitting students, China adopts the form of voluntary filling. First, the provincial education Ministry demarcates three criteria according to the top 20%, 60% and 90% of students' scores. Those who apply for college first have complete freedom. Due to the influence of the traditional idea that vocational schools are often inferior to ordinary colleges and universities, most of the students who are left for the third period only have vocational schools and specialized schools. Even if a few undergraduate school places are left, they will be frantically grabbed by everyone (Lai, 2009; Li, 2006; Sha, 2002; Wang & Ding, 2012; Yang, 2006; Yuan & Chai, 2016; Zhao, 2006).

In China, the object of vocational and vocational examination enrollment is mainly the students ranked at the bottom of the batch under the unified examination enrollment mode. Although there are examination and enrollment modes such as spring college entrance examination, independent enrollment, registration and enrollment, the unified examination mode based on the college entrance examination and the high school entrance examination still occupies the dominant position. As a different type of education mode at the same level as general education, vocational education is often regarded by the public as a specialized education under general education, which seriously restricts the development of Education and economy in China. The problems existing in the development of vocational education largely stem from the fact that China has not formed a perfect independent vocational education examination and enrollment system, and the classified examination and enrollment system is the key point to realize the cultivation of different talents. Through the comparative study on Japan, Germany, Britain and the US system of vocational education enrollment examination, one can come to the conclusion that the current world developed country vocational colleges exam basically has an open admissions policy, certificate system and XuanBaZhi three types: the American community college is a typical open admissions policy, implement "registered" way of enrollment system; Japan and Germany adopt the unified examination or "dual system" vocational education mode, and select the best students who meet the conditions; The United Kingdom, on the other hand, is based on the "national qualification framework" and implements the certification system from bottom to top.

6.3 Challenges of Vocational Education Examination

6.3.1 Lack of Independent Examination and Enrollment Mode

At present, China's vocational education examination is still mainly dependent on the high school entrance examination and the college entrance examination. In the eyes of the public, vocational education is regarded as a specialized level under the general education, rather than a category independent of the general education. In the process of examination and acceptance, vocational education, and ordinary education to take the same test and admissions standards for talent selection, all students unified registration, unified exam, unifies the recruitment of students, the school eventually partial admission, this mode of immobilized stifles the particularity of vocational education, also has restricted the development of social economy and education. Throughout the world's developed countries system of vocational education, vocational education is equivalent to the category of the general education for the students' recognition, and even in some countries, the number of students who choose to enter vocational education is far better than the normal education, and the social economy in these countries often are among the best in the world, which also benefited from vocational education to economic role in promoting. At present our country has many scholars who have realized that using the unified examination system of adverse influence on the development of vocational education, thought to be based on the characteristics of vocational education, will be to test content, mode, admission criteria, such as separated from ordinary colleges and universities, but specifically what respect, how to change, still need to constantly research and explore. Vocational colleges also have obstacles in the process of enrollment, which is embodied in the few channels of enrollment and the lack of guarantee of enrollment source. At present, the main channel of vocational students is through the examination, vocational students in addition to through the college entrance examination, as well as through the recruitment of students through the secondary vocational recruitment examination. As China adopts a unified examination system, and the recruitment of students in colleges and universities mainly depends on the results of the unified examination, so the students admitted through the examination are often the remaining students with low scores, which makes it difficult to guarantee the quality of students received by vocational colleges. The most effective way to make vocational education can effectively connect, recruit to meet the characteristics of vocational education students of the single entrance exam, and because the object is the face of the low scores in the examination of high school students, they are weak in basic cultural courses and other aspects, cannot be successfully admitted to higher vocational education. For a long time, the quality of students in higher vocational colleges has not been improved (Fan, 2010; Lai, 2009; Li, 2006; Liang, 2011; Sha, 2002; Wang, 2011; Xue & Li, 2020; Yang, 2006; Zhao, 2006).

6.3.2 Lack of Scientific Matter in Test Content

In 2019, The State Council issued the Notice on The Implementation Plan of National Vocational Education Reform, which proposed to improve the examination and enrollment method of "cultural quality + vocational skills" in vocational colleges. In 2014, Vice Minister Lu Xin proposed to add a kind of college entrance examination for skilled talents on the basis of the college entrance examination. However, although there are many kinds of examination modes in China's vocational examination and enrollment system, the content of the examination is mostly the same, which is still unable to get rid of the cultural theory examination, lacking sufficient skill-based content. Professional skill scores in the process of examination and admission of the weight reflects the importance of professional skill test, the current higher vocational single recruit exam content mainly for professional skills examination + culture tests, culture exam content as Chinese, Math, English and professional comprehensive theory, by the education testing unified proposition, professional skills, be determined by specific professional categories of coupon test committee. But the proportion is very small, the content of cultural unified examination still occupies the main position. Vocational colleges and universities expect to establish an examination and enrollment model with vocational education characteristics, but they only adjust it under the original framework of the college entrance examination and add a little skill-based test, which still cannot get rid of the disadvantage of taking the college entrance examination as the prototype.

6.3.3 Lack of Occupational Aptitude Test

The content of vocational college examination not only focuses on theoretical knowledge, but also lacks sufficient skill-based test and corresponding vocational aptitude test. Vocational aptitude test can judge students' adaptability to vocational education and determine whether students have the potential ability to engage in or learn a certain occupation. Exam admission process is a multi-party cooperation coordination of circulation system, various parts of the system and perfect operation requires colleges and students have a clear cognition of oneself, sex to test the lack of professional ability, make students' positioning unclear about their abilities, vocational colleges cannot choose suitable talents according to their own characteristics, which hindered the enrollment target eventually. Vocational colleges show the characteristics of low participation in the process of examination and enrollment. This is due to the limited authority of independent enrollment of colleges and universities, and the lack of ability and power to set enrollment goals. Since the twenty-first century, vocational colleges in many regions have tried to find a suitable path for vocational colleges by exploring different modes of examination and enrollment. For example, Shanghai's college entrance examination, Beijing's spring college entrance examination, etc. However, the number of students recruited through these admission modes is still limited, and under the control of relevant administrative personnel, the supremacy of the unified admission mode cannot be shaken.

6.3.4   Enterprise Participation Is Not High

According to the Outline of National Medium- and Long-term Education Reform and Development Plan (2010–2020), "the mode of close cooperation between institutions of higher learning and industries and enterprises should be explored". At present, there is no close connection and cooperation between vocational colleges and enterprises in China, and enterprises have not yet participated in the whole process of vocational education examination, enrollment, and training. The form of examination and enrollment in China is mainly arranged by the Ministry of Education, organized and implemented by schools and examination institutes, and the proposition is arranged by the examination institutes. Enterprises do not have the opportunity to participate in the examination and enrollment. Second, the professional skills test lacks the supervision and evaluation of professional enterprise personnel, so it is difficult to realize the real fair admission; Third, the lack of professional guidance, the lack of rationality in the professional enrollment of vocational colleges, the overlap of popular majors and characteristic majors and the lack of attraction of characteristic majors results in serious bipolar enrollment. The concept of integration between industry and education is the core of every link of vocational education. As the starting point of vocational education, the examination and enrollment system is the trend of The Times and an inevitable requirement to strengthen the concept of integration between industry and education. As the autonomy of examination and enrollment is gradually delegated to schools, the main body positioning of colleges and universities in the process of recruitment is gradually clear, but the image positioning of enterprises in the process of recruitment is still vague, which goes against the realization of the concept of integration of industry and education in the process of vocational education.

6.4   Suggestions on Student Financial Aid in China's Vocational Education

6.4.1   Improve the Vocational Education Examination and Enrollment System

Vocational colleges should implement the classified examination and enrollment system, break away from the unified examination system and promote the further reform of the vocational education examination and enrollment system. First, the form of "cultural quality + vocational skills" examination should be improved, and the proportion of vocational skills should reach at least 60%. For ordinary high school graduates, vocational aptitude tests should be combined to investigate students' career potential and ability. For secondary vocational graduates, the study was conducted in the form of combining professional theoretical knowledge and professional operational ability, and relevant professionals were invited to evaluate. Second, by exploring the enrollment system of an exemption entrance, colleges can set different aspects of the entrance threshold, to student's grades, awards and certificates holdings or other performances, delimit different standards of admission, students can through the "recommendation" or "school recommendation", submit application to the school, though the interview can avoid exam, after admission directly.

6.4.2 Improve the System Construction of Industrial Enterprises Participating in the Recruitment Process

School–enterprise cooperation is an effective mode to give full play to the characteristics of vocational education, and industry-education integration is the core concept of vocational education development. At present, there is no clear system or mechanism to guarantee the participation of enterprises in vocational education examination and enrollment, and there is no clear identity and responsibility orientation. It is necessary to improve relevant systems and mechanisms, clarify the scope of responsibility for enterprise participation and establish a third-party examination and enrollment evaluation institution with enterprises as the main body, so that enterprises can participate in the college entrance examination in a more standardized situation and further play the guiding role of enterprises. To promote the reform of vocational education examination and enrollment system, it is necessary to improve the recruitment mechanism, to separate the recruitment and enrollment, to do their own duties, to get rid of the traditional mode of provincial education administrative departments and examination institutes responsible for the examination and enrollment and to return the right of enrollment to vocational colleges. First, each provincial educational examination institution should form a special test setting team, which is composed of professional technical personnel, industry and enterprise experts, and professional teachers from various colleges and universities, to formulate special test questions and test standards to ensure the comprehensive and professional level of the exam. Secondly, provincial administrative departments can set up special recruitment coordination committees, which are responsible for professional recruitment experts, to regulate problems arising in the process of recruitment, provide consultation services for examinees, and provide emergency measures for unsuccessful examinees, to ensure the fairness of recruitment and play the role of macro-control. Finally, vocational colleges and universities carry out the independent enrollment system, establish the school enrollment committee, implement the national and Ministry of Education enrollment policies, and formulate the main enrollment rules and strategies.

6.4.3 Strengthen Enrollment Management and Integrate Resources Comprehensively

To avoid blindly expanding the enrollment of advantageous majors, the provincial administrative departments should strengthen the management of the enrollment process and restrict the behaviors such as blindly exaggerating the enrollment scale while vocational colleges have the autonomy to independently determine the enrollment scale and specialty categories. Administrative department at the provincial level according to the scale of colleges and universities, and operating conditions, such as information, determine the upper limit of each college recruit students scale, and the year before the actual scale of enrollment and the scale of its enrollment plan comparison, in view of the actual enrollment substantially below plan enrollment of colleges and universities, measures should be taken to reduce the recruitment of students scale, to promote the allocation of resources to the quality colleges and universities. Universities with prominent advantages and great development potential are encouraged to annex those with small development potential and poor enrollment quality, so as to promote them to improve in competition. The skill examination is highly specialized, and it is also a remarkable characteristic that distinguishes the examination and enrollment of vocational colleges from that of ordinary colleges and universities. The reform of vocational skills can be carried out from two aspects: One is to classify and stratify the investigation of vocational skills. Due to the examination subject's knowledge mastery, social experience, age and other differences should be targeted at different types of people, adopt different ways of vocational skills examination. For ordinary students, we can continue to take the form of "cultural investigation + skill investigation", but we should increase the proportion of skill scores in the examination and admission process, highlight the professionalism of vocational examination, and also take vocational qualification certificates as one of the bases for admission, so as to enrich the diversification of the forms of vocational skill investigation. For social practitioners or other people, we can first understand their career motivation, and formulate corresponding exam content according to their relevant social experience and the correlation between occupations. At the same time, for all the exam topics, the vocational orientation test can be used to test career potential and adaptability to meet people's subsequent development. The second is to establish a unified vocational skill testing platform. "The guidance opinions of the Ministry of Education on Actively Promoting the Reform of The Examination and Enrollment System of Higher Vocational Education" points out that the admission committees of provincial institutions of higher learning should strengthen the professional skills examination for secondary vocational school graduates to be promoted, and further improve the recruitment methods based on professional skills. The establishment of a unified vocational skills testing platform can effectively improve the fairness and science of the exam. The intervention of the online system can effectively avoid the misjudgment phenomenon of manual marking. At the same time, the statistical system can also be used to rank students' performance according to different examination standards, which can greatly improve the efficiency of admission (Fan, 2010; Lai, 2009; Liang, 2011; Wang, 2011; Xue & Li, 2020).

6.4.4 Strengthen School Participation

Schools should actively explore the diversified enrollment system, give full play to the main role in the process of independent enrollment, actively adjust and optimize the structure of majors and establish a sound and perfect enrollment and training mechanism. Specifically, the institutions according to their own actual situation, under the system of "classified examination" explore the diverse recruitment way, while completing the independent admission examination alone, perfect "by discussion application" and "registered" recruit students, establish recommended admission system, aimed at students with excellent academic performance to "preferential enrollment policy". Schools should improve the social understanding of vocational education, guide the direction of public opinion and change the students' attitude to vocational school from "helpless" to "active". Schools can take the initiative to set up consulting agencies, invite parents and students to attend relevant lectures, and spread the idea that "vocational education is to export skilled personnel for the society"; Through the issuance of relevant questionnaires, to understand the students and their parents to vocational education "distant" reasons, from the root to solve the lack of attractiveness of vocational education problem; To regain the trust of parents of students by publicizing the employment rate and employment status of vocational school graduates to make them aware that entering a vocational school does not mean a dark future; By actively strengthening school–enterprise cooperation and school–industry cooperation, the company image and market demand are used to publicize the school.

6.4.5 Enhance the Participation of Enterprises and Industries

To promote the in-depth cooperation between vocational colleges and enterprises, so that vocational college students can better serve the society, and excellent employees of enterprises can be further trained, to achieve a win–win situation. In combination with the specific conditions of vocational colleges and enterprises, according to the education planning outline of each province, the method of entrusting the training of students by joint school-running enterprises can be tried out. The applicants are the excellent employees who abide by the law, have excellent work performance and strong desire to study again, or the children of employees with certain career inclination to study in the university. The recruitment of vocational colleges involves not only the development of the country, society and school, but also the personal interests of students. Therefore, the recruitment process for students should not be led by a single institution, but a co-leading mode with schools and enterprises as the core should be formed. In his book Strategic Management: An Analytical Approach to Stakeholder Management, Freeman clearly put forward the "Stakeholder Management theory", arguing that what any enterprise pursues is the overall interests of its stakeholders, and that business operators should conduct management activities based on the interests of each stakeholder. For enterprises, excellent talent resources come from vocational education, and enterprises' participation in vocational education recruitment is conducive to achieving a win–win situation.

At present, there are three main evaluation subjects for vocational education examination, one is the government, the second is the school and the third is the major industry enterprises. The fair and scientific evaluation method should dilute the government's dominant role in the evaluation process and give full play to the important role of enterprises in the guidance, consultation and supervision of vocational education examination and enrollment process. Enterprises' direct participation in the examination and enrollment process of vocational colleges can effectively change the status quo of enterprises' passive acceptance of the output of students under the training mode of vocational colleges and change from an onlooker to a direct participant in talent training. Enterprises cooperating with vocational schools, from students and school oriented to two aspects: one is the enterprise as a consultant, for the school to provide the latest trend of current social career development, provide the evolution trend of the future career development, schools can be set on the basis of appropriate admissions professionals, so as to adapt to the challenges of economic development and industrial transformation in the future; Second, enterprises participate as supervisors. In addition to the vocational education examination which is arranged and organized by the Ministry of Education, schools can hold "secondary in-school entrance examination" according to their own conditions. By inviting professionals from related industries and enterprises to participate in the in-school examination preparation, they can provide students with a second chance to enter the school. Specifically, they can participate in setting professional and clear scoring standards to ensure the professionalism and fairness of the evaluation of the exam results; Participate in the design of occupational orientation test to ensure the accuracy and scientific of test results; Participating in the proposition and investigation of examinee interview will facilitate the school to select more targeted talents, and also facilitate the enterprise to select talents who better fit the enterprise culture in the future (Fan, 2010; Lai, 2009; Li, 2006; Liang, 2011; Sha, 2002; Wang, 2011; Wang & Ding, 2012; Xue & Li, 2020; Yang, 2006; Yuan & Chai, 2016; Zhao, 2006).

References

Fan, B. (2010). Rational discussion on independent enrollment in higher vocational colleges. *University Education Science, 20*(04), 27–29.
Lai, S. (2009). The concept and practice of independent enrollment in higher vocational colleges. *China Vocational and Technical Education, 40*(34), 58–60.

Liang, Y. (2011). A preliminary study on the mechanism of independent enrollment selection in higher vocational colleges. *Contemporary Education Forum (Comprehensive Research)*, 20(07), 68–69.

Li, D. (2006). On the reform of higher vocational education examination system. *Vocational Education Research*, 40(12), 6–7.

Li, X. (2017). Changes and reform trends of examination and enrollment system in higher vocational colleges. *Vocational and Technical Education*, 38(34), 8–13.

Sha, Q. (2002). Research on the reform of higher vocational education enrollment and examination system. *Vocational Education Communication*, 20(09), 5–7.

Wang, J., & Ding, X. (2012). Rethinking the reform of higher vocational education enrollment system. *China Higher Education Research*, 20(08), 97–100.

Wang, S. (2011). Higher vocational independent enrollment: the road at the foot of the road. *Education and Careers*, 2011(07), 36–39.

Xue, E., & Li, J. (2020). Exploring the macro education policy design on vocational education system for new generation of migrant workers in China. *Educational Philosophy and Theory*, 52(10), 1028–1039.

Yang, Y. (2006). Higher vocational education entrance examination system urgently needs reform. *China Higher Education Research*, 40(01), 56–57.

Yuan, G., & Chai, Y. (2016). Thoughts on the reform of higher vocational education examination and enrollment system under the new situation. *Examination Research*, 20(04), 27–31.

Zhao, X. (2006). Discussion on the reform of higher vocational education entrance examination. *Journal of Zhongzhou University*, 20(04), 90–91.

Chapter 7
Reform and Development of Private Vocational Education in China

This chapter explores the reform and development of private vocational education in China. The development of private vocational education is a hot issue in the field of vocational education in recent years. Under the demand of labor force in the transformation of economic development, it is of great significance to study the reform and innovation of private vocational education. This paper takes China's private vocational education as the research object, analyzes the literature on private vocational education on "China National Knowledge Network", summarizes the current situation, predicament and countermeasures of private vocational education in China, so as to better promote the research on private vocational education reform. In China, private vocational education is developed under the condition that education resources are short and cannot meet the social education demand, driven by education demand and market economic reform, and supported by the theory of increasing education supply by realizing education industrialization. As an important part of China's vocational education system, private vocational education plays an important role in increasing the supply of vocational education, improving the quality of vocational education, and promoting the reform of vocational education system and mechanism. To some extent, private vocational education makes up for the deficiencies of public education in training talents and promoting educational equity. With the increasing attention and policy support of the state, private vocational education has made great progress. However, as far as the current situation is concerned, private education in China still faces many difficulties and challenges.

7.1 Literature Review

The large population base of labor force in China is of great significance to the study of vocational education. The development of private vocational education is one of the key areas of vocational education research. Since the private vocational education,

© The Author(s), under exclusive license to Springer Nature Singapore Pte Ltd. 2022
E. Xue and J. Li, *China's Vocational Education Reform*, Exploring Education
Policy in a Globalized World: Concepts, Contexts, and Practices,
https://doi.org/10.1007/978-981-19-0748-7_7

the research on domestic private vocational education has never stopped, especially in recent years, the development trend of private vocational education development and gradually industrialization has aroused great attention from all walks of life. Foreign research on the development of civilian-run vocational education in China is rarely involved, domestic research on civilian-run vocational education mainly focuses on the following four aspects.

7.1.1 Research on the Policies and Regulations of Private Vocational Education

Policies and regulations are the premise and basis for private vocational education to survive and develop, as well as the positioning benchmark to guide its development, and an important guarantee to maintain the school order and create a good school environment. Looking back on the development of private vocational education over the past 30 years,

Fang (2008) divides it into germination and revival period (1978–1992), support and regulation period (1993–2002) and legal transformation period (2003–2008). It also combs and summarizes the characteristics of the policies and regulations of private vocational education in China in the past 30 years. At the same time, she also pointed out that "the private vocational education policies and regulations still lag behind the practice", there are many contradictions and problems. According to Li (2015), private vocational school is of great significance in the process of building the modern vocational education system and promoting role, but also pointed out that our country has not yet set up private schools to develop modern vocational education policy guarantee system and a series of existing problems, from property rights, reasonable return, private colleges enrollment autonomy in three aspects to perfect the non-governmental vocational education policy. Zhao and Xie (2016) show that, based on the alliance and belief division of the private vocational education subsystem and the logical analysis of policy changes, since the founding of the People's Republic of China, China's private vocational education has been divided into four stages: reform and merger (1949–1966), hard start (1978–1990), development scale (1991–2005) and improvement of connotation (2006–2016). At the same time by using the theory of advocacy coalition framework (ACF) run by the local vocational education of the People's Republic of China at various stages of policy change mechanism and the process are analyzed, and points out that the inherent logic of non-governmental vocational education policy change is dominant, the government will support economic development, social demand, diverse interests game the result of many factors such as continuous synergy. Based on this, the paper discusses the research and suggestions of the future private vocational education policy. Xu and Fang (2019) and others have summarized the act of the people to promote non-governmental vocational education in our country since the implementation of the overall situation, and discussed the new background of the act of the people and promoted the positive dilemma of the non-governmental vocational education, analyzed its development under the background of the situation, on the basis of the future on how to promote the healthy development of non-governmental education countermeasures and suggestions.

7.1.2 Research on the Funds of Privately Run Vocational Education

Educational funds include educational operation expenses (that is, personnel expenses and public expenses of all kinds of schools at all levels) and educational capital investment (expenses for building school buildings and purchasing large teaching equipment), which are indispensable financial conditions for running a school. In the early days of reform and opening up, in order to solve the problem of lack of educational funds, the country called on social forces to "donate money to run schools" or "raise funds to run schools", and the private vocational education began to bud. With the promulgation and implementation of the People's Promotion Law, the policy system of education funds and tax adjustment is also under construction. However, in recent years, the scale of private secondary vocational education has been declining year by year. Although the overall development trend of private higher vocational education is good, there are also many local problems. Liu (2003) asserts that for a long time the secondary vocational education in our country has summarized different school funding sources of investment, and points out the existing national secondary vocational education investment insufficiency, the enterprise investment polarization of the fiscal appropriation, the non-state-owned enterprises, pay less, inadequate social forces, and personal investment cost being too high and low rates of return on this basis to discuss the corresponding countermeasures. It also emphasizes the role of the school itself in optimizing the allocation of resources and enhancing the market competitiveness. Zhao (2009) asserts that the secondary vocational education is an important part of high school education in our country, and further discusses that the source of funds imbalance is the key to the secondary vocational education funding shortage, and according to the theory of cost allocation analysis puts forward the countermeasures of promoting education funding sources equalization, that is, improve the government, enterprises, social participation. He (2012) pointed out that at present, the operation of private vocational schools in China mainly relies on tuition income. Under the background of continuous decrease in the source of students, private vocational schools should realize the transformation of diversified funds and income channels.

  Zhou Fenghua (2017) analyzed the funding sources and growth of private vocational education from 2010 to 2015 and concluded that the funding of vocational education in China is mainly from the national financial input; In the appropriation of secondary vocational education, private school sponsors account for less than 1.5%;

Tuition and miscellaneous fees are still the main source of private vocational education income. This paper discusses the reasons for the shortage of private vocational
education funds, and further discusses the development direction of private vocational education under the background of the prohibition of for-profit compulsory
education by the new "people promotion Law".

7.1.3 Research on the Construction of Private Vocational Education Teachers

The overall comprehensive ability of teachers plays an important role in the development of schools. For private vocational education, a sufficient and stable team of
teachers is particularly important. In terms of teaching literacy, Liu et al. (2014) and
others point out a combination of domestic teachers' ability and the abroad application of university of science and technology requirements for teachers' ability to
research on the basis of exploring the modern vocational education system under the
private applied ability structure of college teachers, think the knowledge base, the
professional practice ability, teaching ability and development ability of four parts.
They further pointed out that the personnel training objectives of private colleges
and universities also led to their different requirements on teacher ability from traditional colleges and universities and tried to build a teacher ability evaluation model
of private colleges and universities under the background of vocational education
based on questionnaire analysis and statistical survey. Lu et al. (2020) pointed out
that there are still problems in the identification and training of "double-qualified"
teachers needed by private undergraduate vocational education, such as the imperfect
standards, the imperfect training mechanism and the lack of quality training content.
Chen and Zhao (2021) proposed to prioritize the construction of a teaching team
with a "double-teacher" structure in combination with various difficulties faced by
private colleges and universities, and to do so step by step.

7.1.4 Research on the Establishment of Private Vocational Education Majors

As an important part of higher education, higher vocational education has been
concerned by Chinese scholars. But the research about the private higher vocational
education is relatively few, especially about the private higher vocational specialty
setting. Private higher vocational colleges and higher vocational colleges have similar
professional settings, but compared with public higher vocational colleges, they are
more demands oriented. Zeng (2006) elaborated on some problems existing in the
professional setup of private higher vocational colleges in China, namely, the lack of
in-depth market research and strict scientific demonstration; It is blind to ignore

the existing conditions of running schools; Lack of characteristic majors, focus on low-cost majors; With obvious short-term pragmatism and so on. Liu (2014) concluded that private higher vocational colleges lacked some majors in the primary and secondary industries. The specialty distribution of private comprehensive higher vocational colleges is obviously "emphasis on literature and light on science"; The overall professional structure does not reflect distinct industry characteristics; Some private higher vocational colleges in China do not show obvious advantages of professional agglomeration in their own regions. He pointed out that due to "competitive pressure" and "imitative pressure", private higher vocational colleges in China are similar to the professional structure of public higher vocational colleges, and the role of "complementary function" of private higher vocational colleges is more than the impact of "differentiated demand". The development of private vocational education is mainly based on the promotion of national policies and regulations. The policies and regulations at each stage have their own characteristics, reflecting the characteristics of The Times and the development trend of private vocational education in China in the corresponding period. Related research has also changed gradually in content and method with the change of times. In the process of combing the literature, the author got the following findings. Overall research is relatively weak. In the relevant literature, master's thesis and doctoral thesis are few, in terms of research methods, literature analysis method, historical research method, empirical research method, case analysis method, etc. In terms of theory, only a few studies have involved the concept interpretation and definition related to the dimensions of private vocational education. Compared with "private education" and "vocational education", the research on private vocational education is relatively few, the dimension is still not comprehensive, and the research itself needs to be in-depth; So far on the private vocational education of various aspects of the research, many are higher vocational, private vocational and private universities confused. The privately run vocational education has two characteristics different from the ordinary education, namely "occupation" characteristic and "privately run" nature. The "professional" characteristics require that the teachers have a high level of theoretical knowledge while mastering the practical skills of the major and can effectively guide students to practice training. The nature of "private" determines the absence of financial appropriation for this kind of education, and all the school funds must be self-funded. In terms of the above four dimensions, most of the studies on the predicament and countermeasures of private vocational education are still too broad, and lack of specific suggestions on the development of private vocational education based on the combined analysis of the two.

7.2 Data Analysis

7.2.1 Students in Private Secondary Vocational Education

According to statistics and graphs, the number of secondary vocational education and private vocational education schools in China decreased year by year from 2010 to 2019, while the enrollment and enrollment of the former rebounded in 2019. From 2010 to 2015, the enrollment and enrollment of private secondary vocational education decreased year by year, and increased year by year since 2016. Until 2019, the enrollment and enrollment of private secondary vocational education increased by 190,600 and 410,100, respectively, compared with 2015, while the number of schools decreased by 330. Enrollment and enrollment of private vocational education in the national proportion gradually increased from 2015 to 14.99% and 14.23%, respectively, in 2019, up 4.15% and 3.43% from the lowest point, even exceeding the data in 2010. The proportion of the number of schools in all secondary vocational schools in China also increased slightly. Reached 19.70%. At the same time, from 2010 to 2016, the average school size of both the national secondary vocational school and private secondary vocational school gradually decreased and began to expand again from 2017. Although the average school size of private secondary vocational school is generally smaller than that of the national secondary vocational school, the gap between the two is narrowing, accounting for 72.26% in 2019. From 010 to 2019, the number of schools, enrollments and students in national and private higher vocational education showed a fluctuating upward trend on the whole. By 2019, the number of schools, enrollment and students in private higher vocational education increased by 19, 446,900 and 741,000 compared with 2010, respectively. From 2017 to 2018, the number of national and private higher vocational education schools increased significantly, increasing by 30 and 10, respectively. At the same time, the proportion of the number of private higher vocational education schools in the national higher vocational education showed a trend of fluctuation and decline, while the number of enrollment and the number of students declined from 2014 to 2016, but the overall proportion showed an upward trend. By 2019, the number of private vocational schools, the number of students and the number of students accounted for 22.63%, 22.51% and 21.07% of the national total, respectively.

7.2.2 Teachers in Private Secondary Vocational Education

The proportion of full-time teachers in private secondary vocational schools is generally lower than that of national secondary vocational schools, about 10 percentage points lower on average, and the ratio of students to teachers is also higher than that of national secondary vocational schools. It decreased year by year from 2010 to 2015, and fluctuated upward from 2016, with a decline compared with 2010 on the whole. However, relative to the national secondary vocational schools, the gap has

gradually widened, from 3.28% in 2010 to 8.98% in 2019. In 2019, the student–
teacher ratio of private secondary vocational schools was 27.91:1, which is still far
from the requirement of 20:1 stipulated in the "Standard for Setting Secondary Vocational Schools". Since the statistics in 2016, the proportion of full-time teachers in
private higher vocational colleges has been increasing year by year, reaching 72.28%
in 2019, and the gap with national higher vocational colleges is gradually smaller,
with an average difference of about 1.5%. There are 10 provinces with more than
300 secondary vocational schools, namely Hebei, Shanxi, Anhui, Jiangxi, Shandong, Henan, Hunan, Guangdong, Sichuan and Yunnan. Among them, Hebei, Shandong, Hunan, Guangdong and Sichuan have more than 400 secondary vocational
schools. Seven provinces—Beijing, Tianjin, Shanghai, Hainan, Tibet, Qinghai and
Ningxia—have fewer than 100. Meanwhile, eight provinces—Hebei, Shanxi, Anhui,
Shandong, Henan, Hunan, Guangdong and Sichuan—have more than 90 private
secondary vocational schools, while seven provinces—Beijing, Tianjin, Shanghai,
Tibet, Qinghai, Ningxia and Xinjiang—have less than 10 private secondary vocational schools. There are 5 provinces where private secondary vocational schools
account for more than 30%, namely Liaoning, Anhui, Hunan, Hainan and Sichuan. In
Hunan, Hainan and Sichuan, private secondary vocational schools account for more
than 40% of secondary vocational schools. Tianjin, Shanghai, Xizang and Xinjiang
were below 10%. In general, the number of secondary vocational schools is affected
by the level of local economic development, relevant policies and cultural concepts,
the regional development is uneven, and the lack of effective support and unified
control; Except for some regions, the proportion of private secondary employment
in most provinces is between 20 and 30%, and the private composition is still low.
On the whole, the number of enrollment and the number of students and the number
of secondary vocational schools in different regions are positively distributed; At
the same time, the number of secondary vocational schools and the average size
of schools in different regions also have great differences, mainly including the
following categories: Small number and school places of large scale (jiangsu, hainan,
shaanxi, qinghai, ningxia), the school which has more than the relatively small size
with places (hebei, henan, hunan, etc.), the school and less places are small scale
(Beijing, Shanghai and Tianjin), more schools and places on a larger scale (shandong, anhui, yunnan, etc.), The development mode and level of secondary vocational
education vary greatly among provinces. The proportion of full-time teachers in
the overall secondary vocational schools is 70%~80%, in Jiangsu, Zhejiang, Anhui,
Fujian, Chongqing, Yunnan, Xizang, Gansu and other regions, the proportion of full-
time teachers is relatively high, more than 80%, while Beijing, Shanghai, Hainan is
less than 70%, at the same time secondary vocational institutions and the number of
teachers and staff are too small; In contrast, there are also such as Tibet, Qinghai,
Ningxia and other staff are small, but full-time teachers accounted for a relatively
high situation. In Beijing, Tianjin, Jilin, Shanghai, Hainan, Tibet, Gansu, Qinghai
and Ningxia, the number of higher vocational colleges is less than 30. In Tibet,
Hainan, Gansu and Ningxia, the number of higher vocational schools fluctuates
around 10, indicating that higher vocational education is obviously weak. In other
regions, the overall number of colleges ranges from 40 to 70, with the highest number

of higher vocational colleges in Jiangsu, Anhui, Shandong, Henan, Guangdong, Hunan, Sichuan and other regions, all exceeding 70. In terms of the average school size, except for Beijing, Qinghai, Tibet and other four provinces, which are smaller (less than 5,000), most of the other regions are distributed between 6,000 and 12,000 students, among which Shandong, Henan and Guangxi have the highest average school size, close to 14,000 students (Chen & Zhao, 2021; Fang, 2008; He, 2012; Li, 2015; Liu, 2003, 2014; Liu et al., 2014; Lu et al., 2020; Xu & Fang, 2019; Zeng, 2006; Zhao, 2009; Zhao & Xie, 2016; Zhou, 2017).

7.3   Challenges of Private Vocational Education in China

As an important part of private education, private vocational education in our country in the past 19 years to get a degree of development, can be seen from sorting data: first, the number has been on the decline of secondary vocational education institutions, private secondary vocational teachers is still weak, but the size of its places and admissions from around 2016 to achieve the substantial increase; Second, the overall development trend of higher vocational education in China is good. Private higher vocational education develops rapidly, and the gap between the scale and the allocation of teachers in public schools is gradually narrowed. Third, the proportion of private secondary and higher vocational education in the scale of national secondary and higher vocational education has increased greatly; Fourth, the construction of middle and higher vocational education in some provinces and regions has achieved initial results, and vocational education has been incorporated into the local education system, which has gained certain development experience and foundation. The following is an overview of the advantages and problems encountered in the development of private vocational education in the construction of vocational education system. In the course of the development of vocational education in China, private vocational education, with its characteristics of close to the market, flexible mechanism, diversified forms and efficient operation, has played a huge role in improving the quality of workers, cultivating skilled talents and better meeting the multi-level and diversified demands of economic and social development for vocational education. The advantages of the privately run vocational education depend on and focus on its market orientation, flexible school-running mechanism and corresponding management system determined by the nature of "privately run" and "vocational education", but the experience of various development modes still revolves around the "market orientation". Therefore, based on the motivation and goal of market orientation, the author summarizes the key points of the development of private vocational education in three aspects.

7.3.1 Talent Training Meets Market Demand

One of the common characteristics of private vocational colleges is that they flexibly and actively adapt to the market demand, set up majors according to the demand of the talent market, and have greater freedom of control in the setting of majors and the allocation of enrollment, while most public colleges are limited in this aspect. The majors offered by private higher vocational colleges are mainly based on social application and technical skills, and pursue the dislocation of the training of social senior professional talents, and strive to form their own characteristics and advantages in a certain subject; Relatively speaking, public colleges and universities undertake the task of cultivating talents for the long-term development of the country and society, and pursue "large and comprehensive" and "comprehensive" majors, but they are relatively weak in cultivating vocational talents. On this basis, the professional structure established by private vocational colleges according to the information of the talent market can meet the needs of the labor market, so it has strong vitality and can meet the needs of the talent market of the local emerging industries.

7.3.2 Diversified Educational Mechanisms

Relying on enterprises and service industries, school–enterprise combination, school–school cooperation and jointly holding brand majors are another specific manifestation of market orientation in the development of private vocational colleges. The private vocational education was born in the market and closely connected with the market. Some private vocational colleges are run by enterprises, so they are more familiar with the employment needs of enterprises and better able to find market "niches" than public vocational colleges. In order to obtain timely market information, introduce professional training resources and improve employment rate and educational investment attraction, the other part of schools founded by non-enterprises also need to continuously tap in-school educational resources and enterprise educational resources. At present, the most common way is to establish long-term cooperative relationship with enterprises, that is, to use enterprise funds and facilities to cultivate professional and skilled personnel needed by enterprises, which also ensures the "seamless connection" between the cultivated talents and the positions of enterprises. And some colleges and universities with foreign institutions to sign joint operation, mutual recognition of credits and other agreements, by the international brand to expand influence (Chen & Zhao, 2021; He, 2012; Liu, 2014; Liu et al., 2014; Lu et al., 2020; Zeng, 2006; Zhou, 2017).

7.3.3 Management System and Teachers' Characteristics

From the perspective of leadership and management system, most of the private vocational colleges carry out the principal responsibility system under the leadership of the board of directors, which has relatively centralized administrative power, efficient and simple decision-making, and can make timely and sensitive response to the market demand. However, under the nature of market economy, private vocational colleges can also implement real performance distribution for workers, and accurately evaluate school-level managers, middle-level cadres and teachers according to their work performance, effectively stimulating the enthusiasm of teachers and staff. In terms of teachers, as most privately run vocational schools rely on the cooperative relationship between schools and employers to cultivate talents, the proportion of practical courses in the teaching process often exceeds that of theoretical teaching, which determines that their teaching staff are mainly "double-qualified" (teachers with professional titles and professional skills) teachers. On this basis, most colleges and universities actively promote employment orientation, attract students through high employment rate, and at the same time enhance strength and improve the quality of running schools, thus forming a virtuous circle.

The source of students is the basic prerequisite for the survival and development of vocational colleges. At present, the dilemma faced by private vocational colleges is mainly the "traditional dilemma" of vocational education. The first is the quantitative dilemma. Research shows that the birth rate and natural growth rate of China's population show an obvious downward trend, and the decline in the birth rate and natural growth rate will lead to a decline in the number of school-age children, thus affecting the number of middle school and high school graduates. This means that the scale of "traditional source of students" of China's vocational colleges will gradually shrink, that is, the number of "traditional source of students" that vocational colleges can recruit is getting smaller and smaller, which has a more obvious impact on the utilization rate of running resources and running income of private vocational colleges. In addition, by analyzing the nature of the schools themselves, most of the vocational schools are less attractive than ordinary and ordinary undergraduate schools. At the same time, people in vocational schools have higher recognition of the quality of public schools, and private vocational schools are facing double challenges in publicity and enrollment. From the perspective of the audience, students and parents themselves do not have a high degree of recognition of vocational education, and even hold an attitude of rejection; Compared with public colleges and universities, private schools are also prone to problems such as confusion of management, lack of teachers and unsmooth channels for admission. Therefore, including those that are suitable for the high score students "skills become" road, many students' preference to the ordinary high school and ordinary undergraduate course colleges and universities attended, on to the ordinary undergraduate course colleges and universities or be able to go abroad to study, most of them will not choose to receive vocational education, or give me talk about the private vocational education school. Second, the quality dilemma. The "traditional source of students" that private vocational colleges can recruit mainly include junior high school graduates, fresh graduates, previous junior high school graduates, etc. There is no requirement for the minimum admission score line when recruiting students, and the source of students always lies in the bottom half of the results of the middle and high school entrance examination, which leads to the low quality of the source of students. In addition, there is a big gap with expectations in aspects such as cultural theoretical basis, skill accomplishment and behavior habits, which also poses a great challenge to the cultivation of technical talents.

As can be seen from the previous statistical data, there is a certain gap between the number of teachers in private secondary vocational schools and the national average level in recent years, while private vocational colleges have relatively good development, but there are still problems in the specific structure and quality; In addition, it is urgent to explore and experiment the teaching staff construction of applied undergraduate universities in the early stage of development. In most private vocational colleges, weak teachers are still one of the most obvious problems, the problem is mainly in both quantity and quality. In terms of quantity, private vocational colleges are generally faced with difficulties in recruiting new teachers and great talent mobility. As a result, private vocational colleges cannot attract and retain teachers, which leads to a certain scale of quantity. The direct factor that leads to this situation is that the status of teachers in private vocational colleges is much lower than that in public ones. Although policies and regulations focus on improving this gap, for example, Article 28 of the New People's Promotion Law stipulates that "teachers and educates of private schools have the same legal status as teachers and educates of public schools"; It is also mentioned in the Outline of National Medium- and Long-term Education Reform and Development Plan (2010–2020) that "private schools, students and teachers shall have equal legal status with public schools, students and teachers according to law". But in practice, enforcement and effectiveness have been limited. For example, the channels of teachers' professional titles in private vocational colleges are not smooth, and the mechanisms of entry and outflow are blocked at various levels. At the same time, due to the difference of training and assessment system, the length of service and teaching often cannot be continuously calculated, so that the private school teachers transferred to the public, the cost is huge. These institutional problems make it difficult for private colleges to improve their status in real life, resulting in a lack of guarantee for the quantity and quality of teachers. In general, teachers' in-service income, social security, retirement treatment, working environment and other aspects of private vocational schools are lower than those of public schools, which hinder them from organizing quality and quantity of teachers (Chen & Zhao, 2021; Liu, 2014; Liu et al., 2014; Lu et al., 2020; Zeng, 2006; Zhou, 2017).

As for the construction of high-quality teachers, from the perspective of the quality of teachers themselves, the construction of teachers is largely subject to the subjective factor of teachers' own quality. Professional quality, teaching ability and practical skills are the most basic requirements of teachers in vocational education. However, at present, most of the vocational teachers are still graduated from ordinary colleges,

lack of practical experience in enterprises, and grasp the law of vocational education and the growth law of vocational education students is weak, so it is difficult
to meet the requirements of vocational education personnel training. Second, the
current teacher management system of private vocational schools is still not perfect,
especially for the selection and training of relevant teachers, flow management and
the policies and regulations mentioned above, there is a big gap with the teachers of
ordinary education institutions. Third, the former two factors lead to the irrational
structure of the teaching staff, such as the age structure of young and middle-aged
teachers, the educational structure of full-time teachers with master's degree or above,
the majority of teachers' professional titles are generally low, and the proportion of
"double-qualified" teachers is far from the standard. Among them, the total number
of teachers in higher vocational colleges and private application-oriented colleges
seems to be sufficient, but the unreasonable ratio of students and teachers caused by
factors such as enrollment expansion and difficulties in teacher introduction is more
prominent.

For a long time, most of our educational funds have been invested in general
education. In recent years, although the state has increased the funding input to
public higher vocational colleges, with the per-student allocation reaching 12,000 in
most regions, and a large number of special construction funds such as infrastructure,
teachers and professional construction, there is no obvious benefit to private colleges.
The fund composition of a privately run vocational school includes: Budget of public
finance education funds (education grants+other funding) construction expense, at
all levels of government to impose taxes for education (educational expenses to
add additional+local education of local education funds, etc.), investment, business
income (mainly tuition and fees) by the sponsor (s), school-run industries and business income funds for education, such as income and other income of seven parts.
From the perspective of composition proportion, at present, the national financial
appropriation standard for private vocational education is relatively low, and the
operating cost per student is generally lower than that of ordinary education and
public vocational colleges. This differentiated treatment leads to the situation that
private vocational education mainly depends on tuition fees to survive. In this context,
on the one hand, the sustainable development of the school is easily affected by the
external environment, resulting in a lack of long-term planning; on the other hand,
when the school funds to make ends meet, prone to collect fees in disorder behavior,
and adjust the tuition increase school income affects the enter oneself for an examination rate and the quality of students, and most of the private vocational colleges and
was therefore not easy to raise the ideal number of the construction costs, or at the
same time of guarantee fee income is difficult to maintain appropriate recruitment of
students scale. Besides tuition fees, the investment of the sponsor is still very small,
less than 13% at the highest, and the funds for education from social donations, the
income from the school-run industry and the income from the school's operation
are almost negligible. The lack of funds leads to the serious lag of investment in
the construction of teachers, laboratories and training bases in private vocational
colleges, and the gap between the development level of private vocational colleges
and public vocational colleges is becoming larger and larger. Worthy of reflection,

vocational education, as a type of education from the market for resources ability, should have more social capital into the field, in fact, lack of social capital attraction, it is compulsory education field to attract more investors to enter. In Xinmin, the law that banned for-profit compulsory education background is being promoted and how to guide private vocational education into the market needs more attention (Chen & Zhao, 2021; He, 2012; Liu, 2003, 2014; Liu et al., 2014; Lu et al., 2020; Xu & Fang, 2019; Zhao, 2009; Zhou, 2017; Zeng, 2006).

7.4 Suggestions on Private Vocational Education in China

According to the data and the three key problems of private vocational education, the author puts forward the following countermeasures and suggestions after analysis. Under the influence of the decrease of the school-age population, the enrollment of ordinary undergraduate colleges, the flow of "going abroad fever" (not discussed under the epidemic situation), and the low degree of recognition of vocational education by students and their parents, the quantity and quality of the "traditional source of students" of private vocational colleges have both declined and fallen into a dilemma. In this regard, the most obvious response trend is to broaden the scope of the source of students and improve the quality of the source of students, mainly by encouraging traditional students to apply for an examination, enhancing their willingness to choose schools, transferring two or three sources of students into higher vocational colleges, expanding the enrollment of social students and other ways.

7.4.1 Strengthen the Willingness of Traditional Students to Choose Schools

To strengthen the willingness to choose schools is to improve the attractiveness of private vocational education by popularizing the concept and importance of vocational education, improving the status of vocational education, optimizing the corresponding talent training system and improving the quality of talent training. The first point is that the government and relevant departments need to guide and publicize, distribute support for private vocational colleges and increase jobs in corresponding industries to ensure employment rate. Second, the national recognition of vocational education is not high, a large part of the reason is that there is no perfect vocational skills evaluation mechanism; In the absence of a proper vocational skills evaluation system, it is difficult to quantify the performance of skills, like the scores of college entrance exams or academic qualifications. To solve this problem, on the one hand, it is necessary to establish a skill qualification framework at the national level, classify workers' skills and correspond them with their academic qualifications, and improve social recognition of skilled workers. On the other hand, it is necessary to perfect the current skill evaluation system and use the skill evaluation system to get through the upward path of vocational education. Finally, the core content of the talent training system is major and course setting. To improve the quality of talent training, it is necessary to change the current situation that major features are not obvious and only pay attention to short-term gains without forming high-quality professional construction. Private vocational colleges should give full play to the flexible advantages of market orientation and set up majors for positions in shortage or emerging industries, which are developed in a mismatch with public vocational colleges, so as to form characteristics and advantages in a particular major. In terms of curriculum, according to the requirements of technical fields and vocational positions (groups), based on job tasks and relevant vocational qualification standards, professional courses should be constructed that meet the needs of enterprises and industry standards, and teaching content that meets the needs of positions should be optimized. In addition, on the personnel training mode is still need to consider giving full play to the advantages of the system of private vocational colleges, and further practice of "university-enterprise cooperation and work-integrated learning" cultivation mode, actively explore cooperation in running schools with the enterprise cooperation, cooperation in education, employment, flexible cooperation development of managerial mechanism, formation order cultivation, modern apprenticeships and other personnel training mode, The objective of consolidating the employment orientation of vocational education is attractive with its special nature.

7.4.2 Transfer Two or Three Students into Higher Vocational Colleges and Expand the Enrollment of Social Students

When considering the possibility of expanding enrollment outside the traditional source of students, the target is mainly focused on the two or three students within the school age and the social students outside the school age. Li keqiang, the prime minister in 2020, presented the government work report for the next two years taking higher vocational colleges to large-scale enrollment expansion in 2019 and continue to expand on the basis of 1 million to 2 million, this for private higher vocational colleges is a relief as "traditional students' difficulties, to overcome the talent cultivation of difficult 'important' opportunity ". After the expansion, there will be two changes in the source of students: Of course, to adapt to this situation, the training mechanism and curriculum reform still need to be adjusted, but, the distribution of labor education resources tends to balance. On this basis, secondary vocational education has long been mainly for junior high school graduates as the main source of students. However, the economic and social structure transformation and upgrading of the demand for high-level technical skills and applied talents naturally reduce the demand for middle and primary applied talents, thus becoming a major cause of the continuous shrinkage of secondary vocational education in recent years. However, this does not mean that secondary vocational education is doing nothing. In terms of students, secondary vocational education can be referring to the idea of higher vocational enrollment expansion, path, enlarging the scope of actively, in addition to the junior middle school graduate students, but also cultivate cultural base, the low level of technical skills of student's society, promote the technical skills of ascension, to make it in technical skills as indicated on the position of employment. In most private vocational colleges, weak teachers are still one of the most obvious problems, the problem is mainly in both quantity and quality. To solve the difficulties of teacher recruitment and retain high-quality teachers, it is necessary to improve the salary and status of teachers in private vocational colleges, and to cultivate high-quality teachers, it is necessary to improve the management system and training mode.

7.4.3 To Realize the Identity of Teachers in Private Vocational Colleges

The survival of private vocational colleges first needs the government to provide policy support and system improvement to create external motivation. In the teachers' benefits, the government should build the external environment conducive to the development of non-government applied colleges and universities teachers' survival, solved unreasonable between universities and private colleges, disharmonious problems, improve the level of policies and regulations, such as system design, is beneficial to non-government applied colleges and universities teachers' welfare policy, improve the guarantee mechanism, to protect the rights and interests, In this way, the attraction of private colleges to excellent teachers will be enhanced, and the sense of belonging and working motivation of teachers will be enhanced. Secondly, the government should revise and improve the system of selection, employment and title evaluation of teachers in private application-oriented colleges. While vigorously expanding the number of teachers in private application-oriented colleges, the government should also formulate and plan the corresponding reasonable teacher access system, appropriately raise the employment threshold, ensure the inflow quality of private teachers from the source and improve the overall teaching level and professional quality of teachers in private application-oriented colleges (Fang, 2008; He, 2012; Li, 2015; Liu, 2003; Liu et al., 2014; Xu & Fang, 2019; Zhao, 2009; Zhao & Xie, 2016; Zhou, 2017).

7.4.4 Improve the Evaluation System and Optimize Teacher Training

When privately run vocational schools formulate and employ teachers according to the post standards, they should avoid taking a "one size fits all" approach to the assessment of full-time teachers and should classify and evaluate teachers according to their characteristics and expertise. Especially for the "double-qualified" teachers who emphasize theoretical teaching and practical teaching and have strong theoretical and practical abilities at the same time, more diversified and flexible evaluation standards should be formulated to distinguish them from the teachers in general education and increase the quantitative operational indicators. On this basis, the daily training of full-time teachers needs to be institutionalized and regularized, and emphasis should be placed on improving professional construction, curriculum development ability, teaching and research ability. A feasible solution is to arrange teacher training to the enterprise practice, and send the young teachers of vocational colleges as far as possible to the large and medium-sized enterprises at home and abroad, adopts the field practice, with work practice, study view, lead the interns, familiar with the enterprise or industry standard, job responsibilities, operating norms, docking process, industry development trend. Deeper integration is to make them participate in the relevant professional production process compilation, key equipment operation and control, quality management and control, so as to lay a foundation for the integration of production and education. As for "double-qualified" teachers, at present private higher vocational colleges do not have "double-qualified" teachers and they still occupy a large proportion, and it is imperative to improve the quality and level of "double-qualified" through various channels. Temporary employment training in enterprises is a common channel to improve the quality of "double teachers", but not all teachers can participate in temporary employment training at one time, a more feasible way is to let some schoolteachers teach, and the other part of the enterprise or other university teachers to hire part-time, team division of labor, and work together to complete the team tasks. In doing so, it will be a transition to our more ideal state. The low appropriations standard for private vocational education is the main reason that hinders its development and leads to the shortage of private vocational education funds. In the process of the government exploring and gradually establishing and improving the financial support policies and regulations for private vocational education, private vocational colleges should also give play to their own advantages in running schools and actively try to obtain funds from multiple channels. First of all, in the establishment of financial education funds under the premise of total spending, the government should, according to the principle of education costs, determine funding allocation, adjustment of general education and vocational education the distribution structure of public education funds, build scientific and reasonable system of vocational education college costs, and on this basis, in the central level and local level set up the special funds for supporting the private vocational colleges. The financial support funds are mainly composed of student per capita subsidy and development special fund. The student per capita subsidy is arranged to subsidize the daily operating expenses of private vocational colleges. Special development funds will be used to support the connotation development of private vocational colleges. Secondly, in order to respond to the call of the central government and the demand of talent cultivation for industrial transformation in the new era, some regions have increased the support for private vocational schools in recent years. Many policies have been announced, but most of them have not been fully implemented, which has affected the role they should play. Therefore, the government should strengthen the implementation of policies; For example, when investing special funds to support the development of vocational education, it is necessary to further clarify the amount and expected results of funding for private colleges and universities and strengthen the guiding role of the system construction of private vocational schools.

7.4.5 Transformation of Private Vocational Schools: Diversified Funds and Income Channels

At present, the operation of private vocational colleges mainly depends on tuition fees, and in the background of the continuous decrease of the source of students, its funding sources should realize the transformation of diversified funds and income channels. Non-governmental vocational colleges should play private, close to the market need, the characteristics of flexible for degree education at the same time, actively carry out vocational skills training, vocational qualification, product research and development, assets management, social service and the way to increase revenue, even in the form of lending to financial and property financing, expand school resources constitute a base (Chen & Zhao, 2021; Fang, 2008; He, 2012; Li, 2015; Liu, 2003, 2014; Liu et al., 2014; Lu et al., 2020; Xu & Fang, 2019; Zeng, 2006; Zhao, 2009; Zhao & Xie, 2016; Zhou, 2017).

References

Chen, X., & Zhao, G. (2021). The dilemma and countermeasures of the development of "double-qualified" teachers in private vocational colleges. *Modern Vocational Education, 30*(27), 218–219.

Fang, M. (2008). Policies and regulations: Escort the development of private vocational education. *Education and Vocational, 20*(13), 28–30.

He, Z. (2012). Current path selection of private vocational education development. *China Vocational and Technical Education, 30*(12), 49–52.

Li, L. (2015). Problems existing in the Policy system of private vocational education in China and suggestions for improvement. *Modern Education, 20*(Z1), 33–34.

Liu, C., Zheng, Y., & Zhang, T. (2014). Research on teachers' ability structure in private colleges and universities in Shandong under the background of modern vocational education. *China Vocational and Technical Education, 30*(24), 80–83.

Liu, F. (2003). China's secondary vocational education investment problems and countermeasures. *Vocational and Technical Education, 24*(19), 20–22.

Liu, Y. (2014). Empirical analysis of specialty structure of private higher vocational colleges in China. *Vocational and Technical Education, 35*(13), 66–70.

Lu, M., Deng, X., Yang, S., & Luo, Q. (2020). Exploration on the Identification and cultivation of "double-qualified" teachers in private undergraduate vocational education. *Contemporary Educational Practice and Teaching Research, 20*(03), 130–132.

Xu, Y., & Fang, F. (2019). Research on the development of private vocational education in China under the background of the new "People promotion Law." *Education and Vocational, 40*(06), 99–103.

Zeng, Y. (2006). *Brief Analysis on the Specialty Setting of Private Higher Vocational Colleges Education and Career, 2006*(06), 33–35.

Zhao, L., & Xie, C. (2016). The internal logic of policy change of private vocational education in China: From the perspective of Advocacy Alliance Framework (ACF). *Research on Educational Development, 36*(23), 15–21.

Zhao, Y. (2009). Research on the structural imbalance of funding sources for secondary vocational education. *Continuing Education Research, 20*(02), 134–136.

Zhou, F. (2017). Current situation analysis and strategy research of private vocational education. *China Vocational and Technical Education, 4*(06), 10–18.

Chapter 8
The School–Enterprise Cooperation in Vocational Education in China

This chapter explores the school–enterprise cooperation in vocational education in China.

At present, with the increasing emphasis on vocational education in China, school–enterprise cooperation in vocational education has increasingly entered the public view and become an important part in the process of vocational education. As an important way of vocational education development and progress, university–enterprise cooperation in rapid development at the same time also faces some challenges and problems. Based on this, I was in for some documents and policy based on learning and understanding to some analysis on the current situation of university–enterprise cooperation, and for the sustainable development of cooperation between colleges and put forward some suggestions.

8.1 Literature Review

To get more familiar with the current situation of school–enterprise cooperation in China's vocational education, I have consulted relevant literature on CNKI, and documents published on the official website of the Ministry of Education, and learned about the policies, modes and existing problems of school–enterprise cooperation. By observing the key words and subject content of the literature, the existing literature research basically starts from the policies and modes of school–enterprise cooperation, analyzes the current problems of school–enterprise cooperation, and puts forward some suggestions for improvement based on this.

8.1.1 Policies on University–Enterprise Cooperation

The state has given policy support to school–enterprise cooperation in vocational education. The Outline of National Medium- and Long-term Education Reform and Development Plan (2010–2020) issued in July 2010 requires that "the government should earnestly fulfill its responsibility to develop vocational education", "establish and improve a government-led, industry-guided, enterprise-involved school-running mechanism, formulate laws and regulations to promote school-enterprise cooperation in school-running, and promote the institutionalization of school-enterprise cooperation". In November 2012, the Ministry of Education issued the Action Plan for Reform and Innovation of Secondary Vocational Education (2010–2012) in time, which institutionalized school–enterprise cooperation in vocational education, including secondary vocational education. The 19th National Congress of the CPC clearly proposed to deepen the integration of industry and education and the cooperation between schools and enterprises. In recent years, the Ministry of Education has actively promoted industry-education integration and school–enterprise cooperation in the field of vocational education. In 2014, the state successively promulgated the Plan for the Construction of the Modern Vocational Education System (2014–2020), the Decision of The State Council on Accelerating the Development of Modern Vocational Education and other documents to guide and support the development of vocational education. In the policy documents, the state also called for and promoted school–enterprise cooperation in vocational education. In February 2018, the Ministry of Education and other six departments jointly promulgated the Measures for Promoting School–Enterprise Cooperation in Vocational Schools, which put forward: "School-enterprise cooperation shall be guided by school and enterprise, promoted by government, guided by industry and implemented by schools and enterprises. Relevant departments of The State Council and local people's governments at all levels should establish and improve the promotion and support policies, service platforms and guarantee mechanisms for university-enterprise cooperation". From the three aspects of cooperation forms, promotion measures and supervision and inspection, this paper standardizes the school–enterprise cooperation in vocational schools, improves the vocational education and training system and deepens the integration of industry and education as well as school–enterprise cooperation. However, in terms of school–enterprise cooperation, local policies and regulations are not perfect. As a social system project, school–enterprise cooperation in vocational education not only needs the strong support of national and local policies, but also needs the guarantee of sound laws and regulations. In addition to the education system, relevant policies should also be promoted by the finance, taxation, industry and people's insurance departments. According to local economic development, political and cultural environment and other factors, local governments should take measures according to local conditions, formulate specific and specialized implementation strategies, and establish a perfect legal guaranteed system. From the micro practical level, there is still a lack of specific and operational implementation rules. Detailed and clear provisions have been made on what functions local

governments should perform in school–enterprise cooperation in vocational education, to what extent enterprises should participate in vocational education and what
responsibilities they should assume if they violate their obligations (Dong et al.,
2014; Huang, 2006; Jin & Jia, 2018; Ma, 2020; Lan, 2018; Pan et al., 2013; Shen,
2015; Wang & Ren, 2015).

8.1.2 Model of School–Enterprise Cooperation

School–enterprise cooperation is the main form of running vocational colleges in
China. According to the different modes of enterprise participation, it can be divided
into "enterprise cooperation" mode, "school-enterprise joint training" mode and
"school-enterprise entity cooperation" mode. At present, the channels, and modes
of school–enterprise cooperation in higher vocational education in China are relatively simple and shallow. Practice and training are generally taken as the most
important form of cooperation, which is also called "enterprise cooperation" mode.
Compared with enterprises, schools are more willing to carry out all-round cooperation with enterprises in various aspects such as practice training, professional
setting, curriculum setting, scientific and technological research and development,
and staff training. Based on this, many scholars have proposed and expounded
some new and in-depth cooperation models in deepening school–enterprise cooperation, improving school–enterprise cooperation mode and improving the system and
mechanism of school–enterprise cooperation, such as "school-enterprise community with a shared future" model, university–enterprise cooperation and diversified
co-construction model for education, "5321" school–enterprise cooperation model,
etc. It also introduces new theories and perspectives such as collaborative innovation
and win–win culture, which makes a beneficial exploration for the development of
school–enterprise cooperation in vocational education. Among secondary vocational
schools, the interaction mode between school and enterprise is the most widely used
mode of running schools. The university and the enterprise choose appropriate part-
ners, negotiate freely, reach a consensus on cooperation agreement, and then carry out
cooperation from the shallow to the deep with continuous innovation mode, including
"directional", "order", "named class", "work-study alternation", "subject research",
"vocational education group", etc. In addition, secondary vocational schools mainly
have schools as the main body and enterprises as the main body of two modes
of running schools. Schools as the main mode of running schools mainly include
secondary vocational schools according to the professional needs of the establishment of "school-run factories". It not only creates material conditions for the school
to expand its education, but also provides a training base for students. The mode
of running schools with enterprises as the main body is dominated by the industry
mode, and most of them are vocational high schools, technical schools and technical
secondary schools. In this mode, enterprises raise funds to set up secondary and
higher vocational colleges according to their own industrial types and set up relevant
majors for the talents needed by enterprises. Vocational colleges can be divided into

three categories: vocational colleges belonging to government industry departments, vocational colleges belonging to large state-owned enterprise groups, and vocational colleges co-built by the education department, that is, vocational colleges jointly built by the education department and industrial departments (Dong et al., 2014; Huang, 2006; Jin & Jia, 2018; Ma, 2020; Lan, 2018; Pan et al., 2013; Shen, 2015; Wang & Ren, 2015).

8.2 Challenges of University–Enterprise Cooperation

8.2.1 The Role of the Government Is not Prominent

The government has not created a good environment for school–enterprise cooperation. As the leader of local economic development, local government should, based on the reality, create a good environment to attract high-quality enterprises, retain local enterprises and create conditions for school–enterprise cooperation among local vocational education colleges. To promote secondary vocational schools to train talents for local enterprises, excellent enterprises continue to pour in, so that enterprises and schools can get a virtuous development of quality cycle. The government failed to establish a complete monitoring and evaluation system. Reasonable and effective supervision and evaluation is an important guarantee to promote and guarantee the achievement of policy objectives. Among the existing policies of school–enterprise cooperation in vocational education in China, the supervision and evaluation mechanism of school–enterprise cooperation is almost blank. There is neither an evaluation of the validity of school–enterprise cooperation policy nor a special supervision and evaluation institution.

8.2.2 Enterprises Have Low Enthusiasm for Cooperation

For enterprises, the primary purpose is the pursuit of profit. However, school–enterprise cooperation cannot bring significant short-term benefits to enterprises, but requires a large amount of costs, and there is a large chance that the enterprise will lose money. Enterprises in school–enterprise cooperation not only need to bear the preliminary planning and preparation costs of school–enterprise cooperation projects, but also need to bear the transaction costs in cooperation, mainly including implementation cost, supervision cost and risk cost. In particular, the risk cost, the adjustment of business direction, the shrinking of market demand, the change of production process and other uncontrollable factors may lead to the enterprise no longer need the talent trained before, thus causing huge losses. In addition, the talents cultivated by enterprises may leave their jobs or change jobs, which not only requires the investment of a lot of resources, but also fails to reap considerable performance results. As a result, the enthusiasm of enterprises to participate in school–enterprise cooperation is not high, and even the "fireplace phenomenon" occurs. The internal driving force of enterprises to participate in vocational education is not enough. Most enterprises which rely mainly on physical labor have a small demand for skilled talents and lack the motivation to participate in vocational education and personnel training. In addition, the management of existing cooperative organizations is not sound, and the cooperative relationship is mostly maintained by emotion. In the specific professional construction, curriculum development and the management of practice and training, most enterprises are in a passive state, the standards and norms of education and training are missing, and the cooperation is superficial, and the enterprises lack the strategic development concept.

8.2.3   Cooperation Is Shallow

At present, the school–enterprise cooperation in most of China's vocational colleges is still at a shallow level, and the cooperation field is relatively simple. Mainly due to the teaching needs of vocational colleges, enterprises only participate in school–enterprise cooperation as a supporting role, which makes school–enterprise cooperation stay on the surface and is difficult to further promote. It is impossible to realize the docking and integration of industry and education, enterprises and vocational colleges, employment positions and professional settings. At present, the scope of many school–enterprise cooperation is still very narrow. The two parties lack necessary resource exchange and talent flow, and have not established a systematic joint education mechanism, which is difficult to demonstrate the effectiveness of school–enterprise cooperation. And as the dominant university–enterprise cooperation of schools, the lack of deep cooperation with the enterprise thinking and to adapt to the enterprise requirements of curriculum system, the lack of a long-term mechanism of cooperation between higher vocational colleges and enterprises, cooperation become a mere formality, difficult to deepen the teaching goal and content of the lack of pertinence, students after graduation still need to post for a long-time practice to work properly. At the same time, the academic foundation and theoretical cultivation of excellent teachers in the school are also unable to realize the transformation of scientific research and innovation, to facilitate the upgrading and transformation of enterprises, because there is no good practical research and development platform of enterprises. Students, as the subjects directly receiving joint training in school–enterprise cooperation, their attitude and ability have a great influence on the success of school–enterprise cooperation. First, in the process of school–enterprise cooperation, some students do not have a correct attitude toward work, perfunctory work, and lack the necessary professional ethics. Second, there is no clear regulation on the content, site safety and working time of students' internship in enterprises, which leads to students' wrong understanding of requirements and affects the effect of practical training. Thirdly, the content and requirements of students' internship and training are not in line with the employment standards of the enterprise and the requirements of the job position. Internship experience cannot be of significant benefit to students' employment. In addition, due to the policy of our country entrance examination, to the students of vocational colleges may be lacking in terms of learning and application ability, cause they can't very well combine the theoretical knowledge and practical operation, plus the lack of enterprise in the process of teaching design, students are more difficult to turn theoretical knowledge and practical skills for good (Dong et al., 2014; Shen, 2015; Wang & Ren, 2015).

8.3   Suggestions on School–Enterprise Cooperation and Development

8.3.1   Improve Policies and Systems

In the process of school–enterprise cooperation in vocational education, local governments and local policies have also played a great role in guiding and supporting, especially for secondary vocational schools. However, most areas of our country lack perfect local policies to support school–enterprise cooperation in vocational education, which leads to difficulties in the development of school–enterprise cooperation. We should promote the construction of the local school–enterprise cooperation legal system, accelerate the improvement of the collectivized school–running system, and improve the incentive system for enterprises to participate in vocational education. Give full play to the leading role of the government, strengthen the top-level design of vocational education system innovation, actively break the barriers between administrative departments, explore the coordination and linkage of multiple administrative departments, systematically integrate schools, enterprises, industries, research institutions and other subjects and various resources to promote school–enterprise cooperation. To refine and adjust the code of conduct of school–enterprise cooperation, we should not only restrict the behavior of the government and enterprises in school–enterprise cooperation, but also put forward requirements for the behavior of industry organizations, schools and students, standardize the code of conduct of all parties in school–enterprise cooperation, and clearly guarantee the responsibility standard of school–enterprise cooperation.

8.3.2   Establish an Evaluation System

It is necessary to establish the evaluation index system of industry-education integration and school–enterprise cooperation, set the school–enterprise cooperation policy and its implementation as an important indicator, strengthen the application of supervision and evaluation results, and set up specialized policy supervision and evaluation institutions. In addition, a complete evaluation system can be established, which can be led by the educational administrative department and jointly participated by all relevant parties to establish an evaluation system for school–enterprise cooperation. Some scholars also put forward that the evaluation criteria should be constructed with diversified integration, fully listen to and accept the suggestions from various parties, integrate the requirements of the social parties on the required talents into the evaluation criteria, increase the dimension of the evaluation criteria, check and accept the achievements of the cooperation platform construction, and give full play to the leading role of enterprises in the evaluation criteria. In addition, the third-party organizations should be appropriately introduced to participate in the evaluation, highlighting the diversified attributes of the evaluation criteria and reflecting the objectivity and authenticity of the evaluation results.

8.3.3 Strengthen Communication and Collaboration Between the University and the Enterprise

Due to the different concepts and needs of the two sides in school–enterprise cooperation, to deepen school–enterprise cooperation and realize the sustainable development of school–enterprise cooperation, communication and coordination between the two sides must be strengthened to achieve mutual benefit and win–win results. At present, the school–enterprise cooperation in vocational education in China is mostly dominated by the school and assisted by the enterprise, which makes the talents cultivated do not match the real needs of the enterprise. Talent is the most critical factor for the cooperation and common recognition between the two sides. The improvement of the quality of talent training is of great positive significance to both sides. Therefore, to make the talents trained by the school become the talents needed by the enterprise, the enterprise should participate in the whole process of education of the school, and the school should serve the production management or service practice of the enterprise, so that the cooperation results can meet the needs of both sides at the same time and improve the quality of talent training. In the process of cooperation, both sides should also establish the core concepts of "equality", "altruism" and "win–win" to ensure the smooth progress of university–enterprise cooperation. Through the observation and analysis of the retrieved literatures, I think that there are not many literatures that analyze the policy level of school–enterprise cooperation in vocational colleges, and their viewpoints are relatively similar. The suggestions put forward are basically focused on improving the policy system and evaluation system. There are few studies and analyses on the model of university–enterprise cooperation, but many scholars have summarized and summarized it from different perspectives and classification standards, which may be due to the needs of different regions and different research topics. At the same time, the current problems of school–enterprise cooperation are also concentrated, mainly in the absence of policies and the absence of enterprises. I think suggestions can also start from these two directions (Dong et al., 2014; Ma, 2020; Shen, 2015; Wang & Ren, 2015).

8.3.4 Classification According to the Depth of Cooperation

The specialty direction of the school is determined according to the needs of the enterprise, and the internship base is established in the enterprise, and the professional expert steering committee and the internship steering committee are established. Invite industry (enterprise) experts, senior technicians and other members of the steering committee, and sign professional internship agreements with enterprises to gradually form an industry-university cooperation body. The school provides consulting, training and other services for enterprises, establishes horizontal consortium, sets up the board of directors, and forms diversified investment subjects. Strive for domestic and foreign entrepreneurs, experts, scholars and well-known people from all walks of life to participate in the board of directors, strive for social-related industries, enterprises and institutions to support the development of the school as a director unit, and establish a professional guidance committee with well-known experts to formulate practical professional teaching plans, according to the classification of post groups, determine the professional ability structure and non-professional ability quality group requirements, according to the needs of the enterprise personnel training. Schools set scientific research and economic research directions according to the development needs of enterprises, and transform research results into technological skills, physical and chemical products, and business decisions, so as to improve overall benefits. Enterprises also take the initiative to invest in the school, establish a benefit-sharing relationship, and truly realize the trinity of "teaching, research and development". In the process of providing various technical, marketing, management and consulting services for regional economic development, the school can obtain first-hand information about the local economic development status and needs, and provide cases for classroom teaching, to combine theory with practice organically. In terms of form, the school–enterprise cooperation mode of higher vocational colleges in China is still in the preliminary stage of shallow level and the initial stage of middle level, and the depth of cooperation is far from the advanced stage of deep level. To achieve effective cooperation, the two sides first need to establish a common goal, only the unification of the goal can ensure the smooth development of cooperation. And in the process of vocational education cooperation between colleges, schools, enterprises and students position each are not identical, to achieve synergies, must first clear a multilateral mutual recognition of unified goal, here, the main goal is to fulfill the task of education, realize the applied talent cultivation, the second is that the result on both sides of the ascension and progress, create economic value, etc. For a collaboration to be effective, what it is intended to accomplish and what results it is intended to achieve should be agreed upon at the beginning of its establishment, with specific targets or metrics. When carrying out school–enterprise cooperation, enterprises should also make clear why they want to cooperate with the school, what kind of talents they need, what resources the cooperating school can provide and so on. Only when both sides can reach a consensus on the goal can the follow-up cooperation be carried out well and achieve effective cooperation.

8.3.5 Active Participation of Both the University and the Enterprise

The effective realization of school–enterprise cooperation requires the participation of both parties, and schools and enterprises are the two essential elements of school–enterprise cooperation. However, the status and role of the two are different in the school–enterprise cooperation, so both the school and the enterprise need to actively assume their due responsibilities, give play to their own advantages, and work together to achieve the task objectives. At present, the school–enterprise cooperation of vocational education in China has the problem of low enthusiasm and participation of enterprises, which also leads to students, schools and enterprises are not satisfied with the results of school–enterprise cooperation. Therefore, enterprises need to improve their influence in school–enterprise cooperation, from the development of education plans to the entire education process and content, actively participate in it, to ensure the effectiveness of cooperation. For vocational education cooperation between colleges and schools, between the two sides will generally in faculty training, school funding, professional construction, curriculum and teaching material development and construction, the quality of talent training and employment in the areas of cooperation, task-based education theory, for the enterprise to carry out the theoretical basis for production practice teaching; Enterprises, between the two sides will generally on the resources, knowledge and technology to improve the quality of employees, the high-quality human resources recruitment, the enterprise brand construction in the areas of cooperation, bear the actual professional basic knowledge and basic skills training mission, provide human, material and financial resources to ensure cooperation between colleges and the actual beginning ability training quality guarantee. From the educational process, curriculum and teaching material development and construction is the focus of vocational education school–enterprise cooperation. First, the two sides should jointly formulate the training standards, revise the training program, build the curriculum system, and develop and compile teaching materials. Secondly, both the school and the enterprise should jointly establish a teaching team to realize the joint education of both the school and the enterprise through professional cooperation (Dong et al., 2014; Shen, 2015).

8.3.6 Follow Certain Norms and Principles

At present, there is not a perfect standard and system for school–enterprise cooperation in China, which also has a certain impact on the efficiency of cooperation. To carry out good cooperation, certain norms and principles are needed to ensure the smooth development and promotion of cooperation. From the national level to the local level, relevant policy texts and regulations should be issued to regulate the process and evaluation of cooperation. The cooperation between the university and the enterprise, as well as other relevant industries and departments, should also follow the corresponding norms and support. For both the university and the enterprise, they should also have full and effective communication before the beginning of the cooperation, discuss the possible problems and differences in the cooperation, and solve them through certain norms or by following the principles agreed by both sides, so as to prevent the cooperation from getting into deadlock and dilemma and ensure the effectiveness of the cooperation. At the same time, we should always abide by the rules and ensure that the rules are binding enough for all parties to cooperate. We should not violate or break the rules without authorization and make them a dead letter. Cooperation under mutually agreed rules can not only improve the efficiency of cooperation, but also promote the results of cooperation from the side.

8.3.7   Better Cooperation Results Can Be Obtained

The results of cooperation can also reflect the effectiveness of cooperation. In school–enterprise cooperation, both sides have different demands for cooperation, so it is also a means to judge the effectiveness of cooperation to observe whether both sides have satisfied their demands through cooperation. A university–enterprise cooperation can be proved to be effective if the project and course can benefit all three parties: the enterprise, the school, and the students. From the point of view of the enterprise, the enterprise hoped that by university–enterprise cooperation to develop the practical need of talents and creative talents, and keep talented people in their own enterprise, create more economic benefits for the enterprise, at the same time, also can by communicate with related professional scholars in the field of cooperation, to realize the technology innovation and productivity improvement, to better profit. Therefore, the results of school–enterprise cooperation can be evaluated from two aspects: whether the enterprise has achieved the recruitment of talents through school–enterprise cooperation and whether it has achieved technological progress. From the perspective of schools, through school–enterprise cooperation, schools can improve their teaching level, promote the integration of the existing theoretical knowledge system with the actual situation, and teachers can accumulate teaching experience to improve their comprehensive quality and overall teaching quality. At the same time, teachers can also find new problems in practice, obtain new inspiration, in turn to promote the progress of the whole theoretical system, and the new technology and discovery in time to apply to practice, improve their knowledge application level. From the point of view of students, and students as the main body, accept the cooperative education of university–enterprise cooperation among cooperation should be harvested over the content of the theoretical knowledge, especially with the actual situation of related knowledge, accumulated some work experience at the same time, whether to stay in cooperation within an enterprise or other enterprises into the field in the future, can more quickly into the state, help your own employment. At the same time, under the special environment of school–enterprise cooperation, it can also provide a buffer and transition for students in the transition from school to enterprise and help students to better integrate into the work and social environment (Huang, 2006; Jin & Jia, 2018; Lan, 2018).

8.4 Challenges of University–Enterprise Cooperation

8.4.1 Improve the Quality of Teaching in Schools

Under university–enterprise cooperation mode, the students can better combine theoretical knowledge and practical skills, learn more in the enterprise and industry to the forefront of technology and theory in practical application, and really go deep into the enterprise and industry, to understand the industry of ecological environment, etc., and operating rules, habits, so as to make the school will not divorced from the facts. Different from pure theory study in school, a line through to the enterprise practice, students can know more about their work in the industry and the strengths and weaknesses, more know yourself, and in practice to improve their learning enthusiasm, prompted their learning objectives more clear, reduce the blindness and improve the efficiency of learning. At the same time, students can also learn by doing through field operation, and improve their professional comprehensive accomplishment and ability to solve practical problems, rather than stay on paper, empty theoretical knowledge but cannot be used in the actual work process, laying a foundation for future employment. For the whole school, school–enterprise cooperation can improve the teaching quality and school-running level of the school. If we employ the traditional means of employing technical personnel to the school and teaching through lectures or short courses, the quality, professionalism and teaching effect of teachers may not be ideal, and the attitude of students may not be serious enough, so that the ideal benefits cannot be obtained. Teaching, and the cooperation with enterprises to ensure the quality of practice teaching, through the participation of enterprises in the whole teaching plan, to ensure that the practice of the teaching content meaning and operability, helps to relevant professional curriculum system construction and the reform and innovation of teaching mode, so as to improve the professional quality of students, cultivate their learning ability, improve the learning efficiency. In line with the "employment oriented" school purpose, and related industry technology application and development closely, to meet the needs of secondary vocational schools and market integration, promote students to become talented, schools and enterprises need to develop together.

8.4.2 Reduce the Cost of Running Schools

Through school–enterprise cooperation, vocational education institutions can reduce the cost of running a school. In schools undertake the task teaching mode, independent schools need to spend a lot of cost to the construction of related facilities, equipment, and set up practice base, as well as specialized teachers or technical personnel to undertake to the student the relevant teaching and counseling, and equipment will constantly suffer wear and consumption, need to update, this undoubtedly greatly increase the cost of running the school. Through "school-enterprise cooperation", enterprises can provide training sites and equipment for schools, and provide technical personnel for relevant guidance and teaching, and discuss teaching content and teaching plan with teachers at the school. The purchase and maintenance cost of some equipment is too high, and not all schools have the funds and resources to buy them to use as teaching AIDS, while enterprises will invest more costs in resources. Students can also have access to more advanced facilities and equipment in enterprise practice, which is very beneficial to improve their operational skills. Therefore, school–enterprise cooperation can help solve the problem of imperfect training facilities and equipment caused by limited funds

8.5 Suggestions on University–Enterprise Cooperation in China

8.5.1 Improve Relevant Laws and Regulations

From the perspective of overall regulation, the state should continue to improve and introduce relevant laws and regulations and build a complete system of laws and regulations to ensure the smooth development of all links of school–enterprise cooperation in vocational education. Party committees and governments at all levels should be strengthened to coordinate the development of vocational education in their respective regions. Local government departments to formulate relevant policies should be combined with actual situation, as a whole, coordination, should be based on the vocational education law to develop a clear responsibilities and obligations of policy, encouraging enterprises to actively participate in university–enterprise cooperation policy and fails to perform the obligation of punitive provisions, ways and means to specify the cooperation in running schools, to promote the development of university–enterprise cooperation. In accordance with the relevant requirements of the National Medium- and long-term education Development Plan, local governments may issue relevant documents and policies based on this to encourage school–enterprise cooperation in running schools and cultivating applied talents. Based on the characteristics and properties of the region and the surrounding industry, a clear demand for talent, effective use and integrate all kinds of education resources, under the government macroeconomic regulation and control and guidance, building high skill talented person's raise between college and enterprise platform, through a variety of forms, diversity of university–enterprise cooperation, form a high-end, skilled, innovative talents cultivation system. We will improve the management mechanism of local planning, industry guidance, state record-keeping and independent running of schools (Dong et al., 2014; Huang, 2006; Jin & Jia, 2018; Ma, 2020; Lan, 2018; Pan et al., 2013; Shen, 2015; Wang & Ren, 2015).

8.5.2 Establish a Monitoring and Evaluation System

The implementation of policy is a systematic project involving multiple links. Reasonable and effective supervision and evaluation is an important guarantee to promote and guarantee the achievement of policy objectives. First, we should establish a perfect evaluation index system of school–enterprise cooperation, set the school–enterprise cooperation policy and its implementation as an important index, and set a complete evaluation plan and index to evaluate the behavior and results of the implementation of school–enterprise cooperation policy by schools and enterprises. To evaluate the effectiveness of the implementation of central policies and regulations by relevant departments of The State Council and local governments at all levels. Secondly, the application of monitoring and evaluation results can be strengthened. We should not only strengthen the application of the evaluation results of schools and enterprises as an important basis for performance appraisal, investment guidance, pilot development, recognition and incentive, but also attach importance to the application of the evaluation results of the relevant departments of The State Council and local governments at all levels as an important basis for performance appraisal, recognition and incentive. Set up specialized policy supervision and evaluation agencies. Shall be formulated by the agency responsible for policy supervision principles, procedures and systems, build the evaluation index, is responsible for policy options, policy implementation and the effect of policy evaluation, supervision, including the functions of the government departments at all levels, all the stakeholders to carry out the university–enterprise cooperation policy effectiveness, and the correction and adjustment, to continue or to suspend the relevant policies.

8.5.3 Improve Supporting Policies

To realize the in-depth development of school–enterprise cooperation, it is not only necessary to give full support to school–enterprise cooperation itself, but also need to constantly improve supporting policies to promote its better integration with all walks of life in the whole society. For example, the standardization of employment system, vocational qualification certificate examination system and vocational qualification certification system can not only improve the quality of workers and ensure the quality of products, but also promote the development of secondary vocational education. In terms of legislation, there are both national laws and provincial and regional specific regulations, both vocational education legislation, also from the business, tax and other aspects of the law. In addition to continue to revise and improve the vocational education law in our country at the same time, still need the company law, tax law, labor law, industrial injury insurance law, and other related legal system to form a complete set of perfect, from the social responsibility, the enterprise management behavior, tax pay multiple levels, such as constraints to participate in university–enterprise cooperation of both sides, and restricting the relevant specifications and other institutions from all walks of life. Ensure that the rights and responsibilities of both parties in university–enterprise cooperation can be implemented in place. At the same time, the government should play a leading role and make it clear that the development of vocational education is the responsibility of the head of the party and government. "Cooperation" requires "overall planning", which in essence is the overall planning of the whole society. We should actively break the barriers between administrative departments and explore the coordination and linkage of multiple administrative departments. Systematic integration of schools, enterprises, industries, research institutions and other subjects, a variety of resources to promote the cooperation between schools and enterprises. Only with consistent goals, coordinated governance and effective implementation mechanism can the national system of vocational education integration between industry and education and school–enterprise cooperation be truly implemented.

8.5.4 Increase Support for Vocational Education

To promote the development of university–enterprise cooperation, we need to improve the degree of attention to the vocational education, adhere to the people-oriented, to serve the social stable development as the core, to promote the employment of high quality as the goal, take the initiative to adapt to the industrial structural adjustment and technical innovation, from various angles such as fund, policy, public opinion to strengthen the support and construction of vocational education. Modern vocational education adheres to the employment orientation, comprehensively improves the quality and results of school–enterprise cooperation, and focuses on cultivating students' craftsman spirit, professional ethics, vocational skills and employability and entrepreneurship through in-depth school–enterprise cooperation. To strengthen the improvement and reform of modern vocational education and training system, teaching mode, talent training and other aspects, enterprises need to be deeply involved in the establishment of school–enterprise cooperation platform. To accelerate the development of modern vocational education, it is necessary to promote the reform of vocational education through in-depth cooperation between schools and enterprises and integrate the structural elements of the supply side and the industrial demand side of talent training in an all-round way with the help of the school–enterprise cooperation platform. Especially today, with the rapid development of mass media and public opinion, in view of the existing concept of emphasizing cultural education and neglecting vocational education in our society, we should especially strengthen the publicity of public opinion related to vocational education to create a good social environment and atmosphere for school–enterprise cooperation in vocational education. The central and local governments provide the social environment and favorable atmosphere for school–enterprise cooperation in vocational education in the form of public social resources. Organize the news media to vigorously publicize the advanced units and individuals who promote school–enterprise cooperation, and enhance the awareness of the industry, enterprises, and all sectors of society to participate in vocational education. With the development of vocational education, people's attitude toward vocational education will also change, and their willingness to join and participate in vocational education will increase. Some enterprises that have not changed their thinking concepts will learn more about vocational education, so as to realize the advantages and significance of school–enterprise cooperation and improve their initiative to participate in and seek school–enterprise cooperation (Dong et al., 2014; Huang, 2006; Jin & Jia, 2018; Ma, 2020; Lan, 2018; Pan et al., 2013; Shen, 2015; Wang & Ren, 2015).

References

Dong, X., Wu, W., & Wang, Y. (2014). Research on school-enterprise cooperation model based on collaborative innovation concept. *Journal of National School of Education Administration, 20*(7), 59–63.

Huang, Y. (2006). Study on school-enterprise cooperation model in higher vocational education. *Education Development Research, 20*(10), 68–73.

Jin, Z., Jia, S. (2018). Reflection and implementation path of school-enterprise cooperation in vocational education under the background of the new era. *Vocational and Technical Education, 39*(34), 53–58.

Lan, X. (2018). Thoughts and countermeasures on the effective implementation of school-enterprise cooperation policy in vocational education in China. *Vocational Education Forum, 20*(9), 33–37.

Ma, T. (2020). Community of destiny: A new vision of school-enterprise cooperation in vocational education. *Educational Research of Tsinghua University, 41*(5), 118–126.

Pan, H., Wang, S., & Long, D. (2013). Analysis of current situation and influencing factors of university-enterprise cooperation in higher vocational education in China. *Higher Engineering Education Research, 20*(03), 143–148.

Shen, Y. (2015). Construction of higher vocational education school-enterprise cooperation talent training mechanism—Based on "5321" model exploration. *Research on Educational Development, 35*(7), 49–55.

Wang, W., & Ren, Z. (2015). Research on the construction of diversified co-construction mode of school-enterprise cooperative education in vocational education. *China Vocational and Technical Education, 20*(18), 49–53.